High Praise for
Achieving the Promise of Information Technology

"The gap between the power and promise of IT and its actual deployment in most organizations is tragically huge—and growing wider by the day. This book is the most thoughtful, comprehensive, and well-documented analysis of the problem I have seen. More importantly, it actually tells you exactly what to do about it and how to plan, manage, and deliver effective transformational projects."

Dr. James P. Ware
Executive Director, Fisher Center for Management and Information Technology
Haas School of Business, University of California, Berkeley

"No band-aids here! Sackman pinpoints four management practices to adopt to achieve major breakthroughs in IT deployment."

Neal Whitten
President, The Neal Whitten Group

"Defines how to establish a supportive context for major information system initiatives. Doing so will increase the likelihood of successful system adoption."

Dr. Jeffrey K. Pinto
Associate Professor, School of Business, Penn State-Erie

"Brings effective cross-boundary coordination into the world of transformational systems development by making project matrix management a required management practice."

Dr. Jay R. Galbraith
Professor of Management, IMD (International Institute for Management Development) in Lausanne, Switzerland, and Senior Research Scientist, Center for Effective Organizations, University of Southern California

"Stresses the need for strong professional abilities to perform broad, complex information systems project work successfully."

Perry Anthony
Executive Director, Institute for Certification of Computing Professionals

"Shows how to use project reviews effectively as part of an integrated management review system."

Dr. Hans J. Thamhain
Bentley College, Waltham, Massachusetts

ACHIEVING THE PROMISE OF INFORMATION TECHNOLOGY

ACHIEVING
THE PROMISE OF
INFORMATION
TECHNOLOGY

INTRODUCING THE
TRANSFORMATIONAL PROJECT PARADIGM

RALPH B. SACKMAN

Library of Congress Cataloging-in-Publication Data

Sackman, Ralph B., 1932–
   Achieving the promise of information technology : introducing the
transformational project paradigm / Ralph B. Sackman.
      p.   cm.
   Includes bibliographical references and index.
   ISBN: 1-880410-03-6 (pbk.)
      1. Information technology—Management. 2. Industrial project
management.   I. Title.
HD30.2.S23   1998
658.4'04 – – dc21   98–9631
                                                              CIP

Published by: Project Management Institute Headquarters
              Four Campus Boulevard, Newtown Square, Pennsylvania 19073-3299 USA
              Phone: 610-356-4600 or visit our Web Site: www.pmi.org

ISBN: 1-880410-03-6

PMI Book Team
Editor-in-Chief, James S. Pennypacker
Editor, Book Division, Toni D. Knott
Copy Editor, Cynthia Grant
Proofreader, Lisa M. Fisher
Graphic Designer, Michelle T. Owen
Book Cover Design, Carol A. Carbone
Acquisitions Editor, Bobby R. Hensley
Production Coordinator, Mark S. Parker

PMI books are available at special quantity discounts to use as premiums
and sales promotions, or for use in corporate training programs. For more
information, please write to the Business Manager, PMI Publishing Division, Forty
Colonial Square, Sylva, North Carolina 28779 USA. Or contact your
local bookstore.

The paper used in this book complies with the Permanent Paper Standard issued by
the National Information Standards Organization (Z39.48—1984).

Dedication

To the men and women who are making the Information Age a reality for their companies ...

Disclaimer

Although the methods and approaches described in this book emanate from extensive research and many years of experience, the author cannot know all the circumstances in which, or how, a company might apply them. For this reason, the extent and kind of results achieved must be the responsibility of company management.

Contents

List of Figures

Preface

During my twenty-six year career with Levi Strauss & Co. I had the privilege to meet and work with many talented individuals in the domestic and international areas of Levi Strauss & Co. and other corporations. By doing so I had the opportunity to share thoughts and concerns about information technology and its deployment in a corporate setting. In many cases, expression of problems they had encountered personally while either working in the systems development field or contributing to systems projects as users gave me insight into common issues and challenges that information technology deployment presents. A further source of understanding has been my eleven-year membership in the Project Management Institute Northern California Chapter (United States), which gave me the opportunity to discuss issues with project managers who led a variety of important projects, thus broadening my exposure to project management outside the information systems field.

About ten years ago I decided to find out why companies and information systems employees have such a difficult time with information technology deployment, especially on large projects, and to write a book about my findings. I initiated a study program that consisted of extensive reading and gaining of professional certifications in addition to my continuing project management and system architect work at Levi Strauss & Co. I truly became immersed in the field, at times to the point where I felt inundated by the data and buffeted by conflicting professional viewpoints. I always had told myself that there is an answer to every systems problem. This point of view must have been what kept me going. In

December 1994 I retired early to study the subject full time and to prepare the manuscript. I came to the realization in late 1995 that the conflict between management practices and the nature of systems work was the essence of the problem. From that point forward the solution started to form, presented in this book as the Transformational Project Paradigm.

I wish to thank the many managers and staff members with whom I worked at Levi Strauss & Co. and at other companies. Their concerns and interest in progress contributed greatly to this book. Please note that no references are made in this book to any aspect of business practices at Levi Strauss & Co. or at other corporations.

My deep appreciation goes to PMI Publishing Division staff members who performed every step of turning the manuscript into a final product with expertise and professionalism. I especially wish to thank Bobby Hensley, who assisted me with document submission, scheduled the steps, and was the main point of contact; Toni Knott, who led editing work, ably assisted by a contract editor, Cynthia Grant; Michelle Owen, who designed the book interior; Carol Carbone, who designed the book exterior; and Amy Goretsky, who worked with me to obtain the review quotations. Ms. Goretsky brought up the possibility of a more descriptive book title and participated in a PMI brainstorming session that produced the main title and the subtitle, which fully captured the goal and content of the book. Jim Pennypacker was supportive throughout the endeavor and set the cooperative, professional tone for all participants.

Most of all I wish to thank my wife, Anne, who has experienced thirty-four years being married to a project manager, system architect, and consultant with all of the ups and downs, challenges, and frustrations that systems work entails. She spent many months away from her musical and artistic interests assisting me with her compositional and word processing skills in the writing of *Achieving the Promise of Information Technology*. Observations about the field from a wife's experience have given the book a broader frame of reference than I ever could have given it on my own.

Introduction

Society, organizations, and individuals are faced with an incredibly difficult task: *how* to convert the huge and growing amount of information and knowledge (technology) and the widely available resources and capital into innovative, implementable, effective, and timely solutions for problems.

Gerald Nadler and Shozo Hibino, *Breakthrough Thinking*

This book is intended to generate discussion and comment at all company levels about management practices that a company must have to support transformational project work based on the nature of systems work. It is written for senior managers who have the authority to revise and employ such practices. The business media, consultants, and the academic community also should be interested in the book because of its bearing on crucial information system development projects.

The intended audience does not include managers and staff members involved in development of software as a product for sale, for example, application package, database, and operating system software; or as a combined hardware/software product. Although these persons might find the text interesting and helpful, the thrust of the book concentrates on deployment of advanced information technology successfully in business-critical application areas.

The book is written for commercial enterprises because that is where my experience has taken place. I believe that many of the principles can also apply to governmental agencies and nonprofit organizations, but I do not wish to make assumptions.

1

In general, the book applies to large and mid-sized companies with 500 or more employees. In some industries, information technology might be used more extensively in companies with fewer than 500 employees than in companies with more than that number.

My work can assist companies to transform their operations and services to the Information Age. Companies can only achieve this goal by optimizing deployment of advanced information technology in their mainstream business areas, such as supply chain management and consolidated financial reporting. Transformational projects that bring about dramatic improvements in work performance are vital.

All required technical innovations, which I group under the term *advanced information technology,* are available now to support transformation—networking, especially in the form of the Internet and its restricted variations (intranets and extranets), huge mass storage, program packages, database software, and operating systems. The term *networking,* as used in the text, includes private networks and all forms of the Internet.

Although most agree that advanced information technology must transform work performance in mainstream business areas to achieve breakthroughs in growth opportunities, productivity, cost control, asset utilization, and customer satisfaction, achieving the desired level of progress has proven difficult. Many companies have tried various practices and techniques that have led only to limited success, frequently in conditions of frustration and turmoil for all involved.

Until now a management practices framework, the foundation for crucial projects, has been missing. The Transformational Project Paradigm (TPP) described in this book can fulfill this need. The paradigm applies to all types of business organization and system development approaches. It is intended to give company management an opportunity to expand successful management practices, instead of having to start over from scratch.

Defining management practices from the nature of systems work perspective, the essence of the TPP, represents original thinking. This simple change in perspective clarifies what company managers can do to solve intractable problems.

Chief information officers and their information systems managers have accomplished much in companies to improve their internal management practices, drawing on their own knowledge and experience and on study done by others. As an example of study, the Software Engineering Institute at Carnegie Mellon University (United States) has developed the capability maturity model for software and the people capability maturity model that are referred to by chief information officers. Improvements made by chief information officers and their managers to their information system areas, while necessary, cannot go far enough. The management practices of the company itself must be supportive of the nature of systems work. That is the thrust of the TPP.

The TPP framework, when customized and detailed by company managers, can become the *context for successful, repeatable transformational projects.* Jeffrey Pinto, a leader in the study of project management, and I agree on the need for a supportive context for introduction of information systems.[1] Pinto dispels the easy answer by some of having the chief executive officer direct crucial, high-risk projects by describing how an in-charge chief executive had delayed a high-speed computer notebook project and pushed it over budget.[2] This does not mean, of course, that a chief executive should not lead a TPP initiative. Leadership must take place, however, within a *context of management practices consistent with the nature of systems work, regardless of the person in charge.*

Unlike prescribed techniques, the TPP framework is intended to be customized and detailed by individual companies. Darrell Rigby, a Bain & Co. consultant and originator of the Billboard chart for management theories, said in a *Business Week* commentary that smart companies tend to customize ideas, win top-down support for them, and devote considerable effort to making them work.[3] The TPP fits this description.

Past single action ideas such as system development methodology, computer aided software engineering, and joint application design have been helpful in some instances, but have come nowhere near the total solution that is needed. The TPP offers a way for a company to review its management practices in light of the nature of systems work, and to make adjustments where management decides it's beneficial.

The four supportive management practices—beginning-to-end accountability, cross-boundary coordination, information systems division home departments, and a management reporting system—flow from the nature of systems work. Unlike results from best practices surveys, field examples from companies are not included in the text. The paradigm, based on systems work to determine what management practices are needed, does not flow from surveys and case studies. The TPP establishes the *why* of supportive practices independently from the *what* done by other companies, recognizing that every company has different needs.

Deployment of advanced information technology through transformational projects can create the breakthroughs essential for company progress and, indeed, in some cases, for survival itself. In order for the paradigm to work, each component discussed in the following chapters is essential to overall success. Omission of one component endangers viability of the entire paradigm.

Part I

The Transformational Project Paradigm Compared to Current Practices

1

The Transformational Project Paradigm

I have for some time questioned why information technology so rarely delivers the promise implicit in the capabilities of the technology. I am now convinced that we must reject the existing paradigms for investment appraisal, specification development, and operation of computing systems. A new paradigm is needed where systems are based on stable corporate infrastructures to allow affordable decentralisation, where application is decentralised, but facilities are shared; where systems are designed more for communication than for automation of self-contained processes; where systems are built expressly to assist the process of change and not to automate current practice.

John Spackman, in *The New Organization*

The Transformational Project Paradigm (TPP) fosters creativity with accountability to generate superior concepts for advanced information technology deployment. The word *concept* as used in this book has a much broader scope than an idea. An idea represents a single thought without regard to workability and interrelationships. A concept, in contrast, is only viable when all related business and technical aspects mesh into a workable solution on a broad and detailed basis.

Edward de Bono, a leading authority on the topic of creativity, maintains that as all organizations reach a plateau of competence, only better concepts will provide competitive advantage.[1] Denis O'Leary, executive vice president and chief information officer at Chase Manhattan Bank and *Information Week* 1996 Chief of the Year, says that technology must be integrated into new business models rather than added to old models in order for organizations to thrive.[2] Superior conceptual ways of doing business, made possible by advanced information technology capabilities, can now be combined into corporate goals to establish a vision for breakthrough results.

Information technology executives saw the need to align the information systems area with corporate goals as the leading issue in the 1997 survey of critical information system management issues by Computer Sciences Corporation. The worldwide survey of 613 information technology executives across sixteen industries showed the alignment issue as the first of nineteen issues in all geographic areas—Europe, North America, and Asia/Pacific.[3] This issue ranked first or second in North America in eight of the nine prior years; it ranked fourth once, in 1990. Patti Prairie, vice president of IBM's Financial Services Industries consulting practice, reports that experience with dozens of clients in the United States, Europe, and Japan is consistent: only companies that achieve effective alignment between business and information technology strategies will maximize the value realized from investment in information technology.[4] Crucial transformational project results must be aligned with corporate strategy. The TPP promotes this alignment.

The TPP framework, *sourced in the nature of systems work*, is displayed in Figure 1.1, illustrating the four key elements of systems work.

Driven by Concepts. Concepts, not requirements, drive systems work in transformational projects. The TPP operating and project concepts illustrate how advanced information technology can address TPP goals and objectives. They tie together under single responsibility the *what* of the strategic direction with the *how* of advanced information technology deployment. The common complaint of spending millions on technology

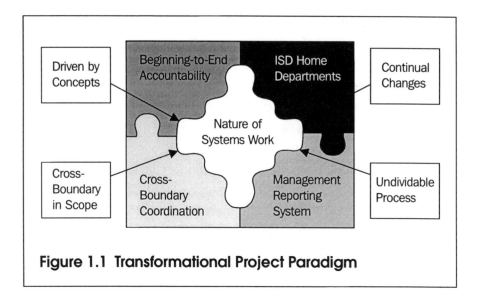

Figure 1.1 Transformational Project Paradigm

without commensurate results often is rooted in use of traditional concepts. Proceeding directly from goals and objectives to requirements—or what the system must produce for users in terms of screens, reports, and processing—*locks in traditional concepts.*

Cross-Boundary in Scope. A TPP initiative can cross function, process, business unit, geographic, and/or company boundaries. Work scope flows from the operating concept and cannot be preset without considering advanced information technology capabilities. Reorganizations, if needed, *should follow, not precede* system development. *Advanced information technology capabilities interact with and enable the strategic direction and should not be confined to enabling reorganized business processes.*

Continual Changes. Requirements, scope, and even concept changes continually beset transformational project work. Change is endemic to systems work because participants learn more as development proceeds. External change often occurs as well. Transformational Project Paradigm (TPP) initiative leaders and project owners must evaluate whether, how, and when to schedule the changes.

Undividable Process. Systems work is a dynamic continuum from TPP initiative goals and objectives through final cutover of the last related system because changes flow in both directions. Moreover, Frederick Brooks, a recognized authority in software development practices, points out that software cannot be described in geometric form the way that land is mapped and silicon chips are diagrammed.[5] A construction architect can express his abstract concepts in concrete three-dimensional drawings, documents that can even be used in court to define the line between architect and construction manager accountability. A system architect, however, can never escape from the abstract. A system design cannot be expressed in length, height, and width.

The dynamic continuum and lack of physical representation prevent clean handoffs. Thus, accountability for conceptual design, scope, requirements, and execution cannot be split for transformational project work. As implied in Figure 1.1, the nature of systems work demands four supportive management practices.

Beginning-to-End Accountability. Good management requires accountability for TPP initiatives, as for any other business activity, because accountability increases the chance of success. When established fairly and logically, accountability becomes a force for progress, not simply a defense against failure.

Cross-Boundary Coordination. All project participants, including functional managers, system architects, and project managers, report to the TPP initiative leader or to project owners on a project basis. Trust and collaboration are crucial to make dual reporting work because systems communication calls for the ability to create in another's mind a common understanding of ideas, issues, options, and constraints.

Information Systems Division Home Departments. These departments consist of system concepts for system architects, project management for project managers, and the development resource pool for development team members. Transformational project work requires staff ability to perform broad and complex assignments. When information systems division home departments (also called centers of excellence) are

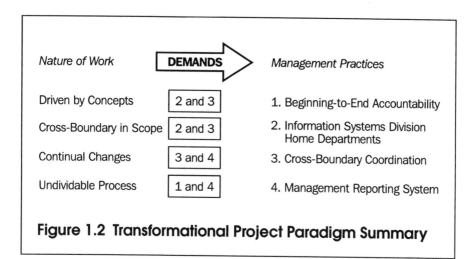

Figure 1.2 Transformational Project Paradigm Summary

organized by speciality, members have maximum opportunity to develop their skills, given enlightened management.

Management Reporting System. The TPP management reporting system makes accountability real. Information technology aligns and clarifies the flow of responsibility from the strategic goals and objectives for a TPP initiative through cutover of the final related project. The reporting system provides for use of the most recent estimate range for project control, not earlier ones that can become irrelevant as additional work details become known.

The four management practices are described further in Chapters 4, 5, and 6. Figure 1.2 displays how the nature of systems work and related management practices are linked. A brief explanation follows.

Superior concepts that cut across boundaries require expert system architects, project managers, and development team members. Home departments foster skill and expertise development; members have a place to return to. Broad concepts need cross-boundary coordination by definition.

Cross-boundary in scope requires flexible assignment of system architects to determine the natural scope of future systems. Project managers execute the projects within that scope and therefore need to be flexibly assigned. Cross-boundary coordination must consist of a strong matrix for TPP initiative leader and project owner authority within an environment of trust and collaboration among all participants.

Continual changes require cross-boundary coordination to resolve issues flowing from internal and external sources. The management reporting system must track disposition of the changes.

Undividable process requires beginning-to-end accountability because the nature of the work prevents clean handoff points. The management reporting system makes accountability real for the participants.

The TPP framework, *when customized in detail* for a company, offers the probability of a high success rate in formulating superior concepts and in executing them through transformational projects. When expanded in this way, the TPP becomes a *context, not an instructive method,* under which systems can be formulated and deployed. Webster defines context as *the interrelated conditions in which something exists or occurs.*

The TPP can become a consistent practice accepted throughout the organization because of the reasons that follow. It applies to any form of company organization. It works with any combination of in-house or outsourced development. It applies to any technical architecture—mainframe, client/server, and network-centric. It holds regardless of technical changes and advances, and it obviates company disruptions caused by forms of reorganization that are not needed at the outset.

Contrary to speculation about uninformed executives, corporate senior managers appear ready to fulfill their leadership roles required by the TPP. The consulting firm A.T. Kearney found in a survey of 100 chief executive officers and other senior executives that 85 percent feel comfortable dealing with technology issues. Sixty-nine percent claim to have a good working knowledge of technologies used in their companies and of the impact those technologies have on organizational performance. Forty percent say that they spend more than 10 percent of their time learning about relevant technologies.[6]

Senior management information technology leadership is becoming an expectation of boards of directors according to observations from five executives who attended a three-day Wharton School of Business Directors' Institute in late 1997. *Computerworld* reported that directors are discussing information technology projects and partners, and demanding that general managers get more involved in information technology decisions and strategy.[7]

The Transformational Project Paradigm in Action

Concept development within the TPP is based on creative, conceptual thinking tested by constructive analysis. Target solutions represented by tentative operating and project concepts are formulated through creative, conceptual thinking. Then they are evaluated through constructive analysis in the form of requirements testing to assure that the concepts will work in practice. Both modes of thinking are required for transformational project work.

Extensive capabilities and large costs of advanced information technology deployment obligate senior managers to lead in definition and structuring of the TPP initiatives. The paradigm offers a structure for defining the action steps to create workable operating and project concepts and to deploy them through advanced information technology, with accountability, to achieve the TPP initiative goals and objectives. The TPP begins with the chief executive-led senior management team establishing the company's strategic direction, or game plan, taking advanced information technology capabilities into account, to define one or more TPP initiatives.

John Rockart, director of the Center for Information Systems Research at the Massachusetts Institute of Technology Sloan School of Management (United States), observed in 1988 that a small but growing number of senior line and staff executives were taking responsibility for significant strategic projects centered on computer and communications technology in their companies, divisions, or departments. He noted that only line management has the power to initiate and execute an organizational transformation of any magnitude.[8] The nature of systems work demands that business area executives lead conceptual change TPP initiatives where advanced information technology is central to achieving planned results.

The TPP initiative is the basic unit, conceived within a company's strategic direction, which provides the foundation for deployment of advanced information technology. A TPP initiative has the following attributes when executed through transformational projects:

- connects with strategic direction goals and objectives
- employs advanced information technology, including networking, to activate it
- operates across function, process, business unit, geographic, and/or company boundaries
- offers dramatic improvement in the way work can be performed through a superior concept to achieve growth, increased productivity, cost control, better utilization of assets, and/or higher customer satisfaction
- produces competitive value for an individual company or for an alliance of companies
- applies to business-critical application areas such as production and inventory control, order management, and financial reporting.

Companies might have several initiatives within the strategic direction, for example, supply chain optimization, sales force automation, a marketing alliance with another company, and creation of a new product line. Of these, only supply chain optimization conforms to the Transformational Project Paradigm (TPP) definition. The others are non-TPP initiatives.

What should companies do that foresee the need for only one TPP initiative? Should they expend the time and effort necessary to set up a supportive management practices context for transformational project work based on the nature of systems work? The answers depend on the need to improve the probability of a successful outcome. Only the chief executive-led senior management team can decide on the level of risk it wants to assume on a crucial endeavor.

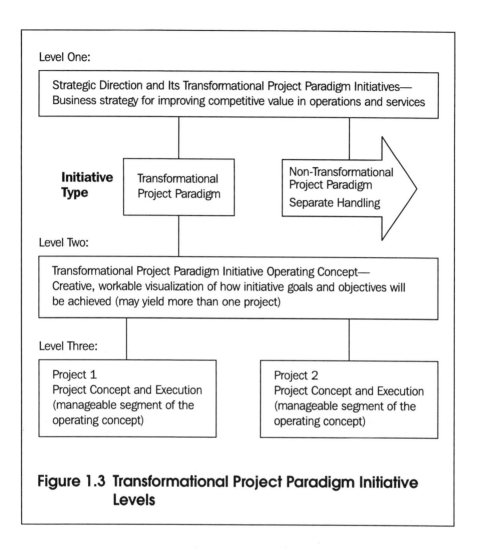

Figure 1.3 Transformational Project Paradigm Initiative Levels

The term *initiative* as used in this book means *a set of related projects.* The word *program* is often used to mean the same thing. I am using the former term because of its widespread use in private industry and to avoid possible confusion with computer programs. Each TPP initiative requires formulation of an *operating concept,* along with definition of an *individual project concept* for each related transformational project.

The TPP emphasizes the *power of the concept and the establishment of accountability.* Accountability begins at the highest levels within a company, and continues at appropriate levels throughout the entire continuum. The TPP recognizes three levels of endeavor, as displayed in Figure 1.3.

Transformational project work is focused on supporting, with advanced information technology, the goals and objectives of the strategic direction by means of TPP initiatives. The TPP offers senior management the opportunity to deploy advanced information technology while maintaining stability in continuing operations up to the point of cutover to the new system *because user personnel reorganization, if needed, occurs after* the operating and project concepts are formulated and project work has begun.

Cutover becomes a time of realistic optimism because participants should know what to expect and where they can fit into the new working arrangement after information technology deployment using the TPP approach. Information systems division and user personnel can have the opportunity to advance in their careers through successful deployment to learn transferable job skills for work in other areas and to retrain for new and different jobs within the affected area. Information systems division team members can increase their proficiency in both conceptual project work and project execution skill areas through on-the-job experience.

The Strategic Direction

The strategic direction, or game plan, is derived from goals that represent sought-after future positions, and objectives that represent measurable achievements. The terms *goals* and *objectives* sometimes are used interchangeably. To clarify their use in this book I am using definitions by Paul Strassmann, former chief information executive for General Foods, Kraft, Xerox, and the Department of Defense:

> Objectives must be explicitly measurable performance commitments.
> Objectives must be measured to determine how near you are to where

you want to be. If you do not have a calculable test of performance, you cannot claim to have an accountable objective. Goals are expectations, prospects, possibilities and ambitions.[9]

The strategic direction, with its initiatives and related projects, is the central control instrument that senior management uses to maintain focus in planning for advanced information technology deployment under the TPP. All work proceeds from this original source. David Cleland, a leader in seeing project management as a way to effect strategic change in organizations, describes his view:

> No organization can escape the relentless pace of change. Out of the threats and promises of such change takes project management from its "special case" of management to the objective of a rightful place as a *philosophy* in the strategic management of organizations.[10]

The paradigm supports *discontinuous change* necessary for a company to make major advances through strategic TPP initiatives and their related projects.

Sequence of Transformational Project Work

Initially, the chief executive-led senior management team will need to resolve issues involved in formulating a sound strategic direction taking advanced information technology capabilities into account. These issues vary from company to company and can be determined and prioritized only by senior management. Among the general topics management can include are: aspects of customer service, product development, new markets, channels of distribution, and operating costs. Senior managers should distinguish between two types of strategic direction initiatives in their planning sessions:

Transformational Project Paradigm (TPP) initiatives operate across boundaries, feature a superior concept, produce a competitive value, are business critical, and require advanced information technology as a central component. For example, a TPP initiative, if its goal is to optimize the supply chain, can have effects on personnel, transportation, facilities, inventories, and product flow—all effects will be the responsibility *of a TPP initiative leader and project owners.*

Non-TPP initiatives apply to all other strategic endeavors—mergers, marketing alliances, downsizing, sales force automation, new product lines, plant relocation, and so forth—not requiring deployment of advanced information technology in a cross-boundary mode.

Two steps should be taken to define and structure the strategic TPP initiatives. *First,* the chief executive-led senior management team consults with the chief information officer and experts in the business application areas to qualify certain broad areas as potential TPP initiative candidates. The chief executive or the chief operating officer appoints members of the team or other managers to serve as TPP initiative leaders and assume responsibility for defining and structuring their initiatives. Geoff Hogbin and David Thomas, consultants with experience in the IBM Consulting Group, describe the search for new applications:

> The creative processes are those that facilitate the search for new applications of information technology to support the strategic direction of the business. They start by asking, "If this is the business plan, then how might information technology be developed to support it?" But they go further and ask, "What opportunities does the use of information technology present? How can we exploit them?"[11]

The chief executive-led senior management team is responsible for targeting the strategic direction TPP initiatives correctly in the marketplace, a prerequisite to success of advanced information technology deployment.

Second, appointed TPP initiative leaders should draw upon the knowledge of potential user project owners knowledgeable in their application areas and of information systems division system architects who have the requisite technical knowledge. *Both* can become valuable sources of workable and effective information for structuring the initiatives. This step should bring high-level user needs and information technology considerations into view to increase the probability that the ensuing operating concept can fulfill the TPP initiative goals and objectives.

The outcome of these working sessions should be TPP initiative goals and objectives that meet the overall purpose of the initiative taking user needs and technology capabilities into account. Several iterations among the chief executive-led senior management team, the TPP initiative leader's working team, the chief information officer, and consultants might be needed to clarify the goals and objectives for operating concept formulation.

The strategic direction *TPP initiatives* determine *what* needs to be accomplished and the anticipated results. The *TPP operating concepts* are conceptual representations of *how* the TPP initiatives will work with support of advanced information technology. Creative, conceptual thinking tested by constructive analysis must be used to formulate TPP operating and project concepts. Individual project results *link and align* with TPP initiative goals and objectives to produce the desired results, assuming that project execution and system cutover efforts are managed effectively.

The Transformational Project Paradigm Operating Concept

The operating concept flows from and interacts with the TPP initiative goals and objectives. A well-formulated, effective operating concept is the biggest lever in realizing payoff from advanced information technology at the project level because it portrays the overall design for transformational project work. The operating concept transcends process and functional boundaries; thus, the conceptual work *must precede* organization, roles and responsibilities, and personnel selection.

The operating concept, the focal point for structuring transformational information systems projects, forms the bridge between the TPP initiative and the transformational development projects required to realize breakthroughs in growth opportunities, productivity, cost control, capital utilization, and customer satisfaction. An operating concept, when fully and creatively developed, gives participants the information they require to understand the TPP initiative in terms of its effect on the company and on themselves. In this way the operating concept can galvanize motivation and support at all levels.

A superior operating concept provides employees with significant performance challenges and opportunities for individual staff member development. According to Jon Katzenbach and Douglas Smith, management consultants and co-authors of *The Wisdom of Teams,* a specific performance challenge, clear and compelling to all team members, is the greatest motivator rather than the answer commonly assumed, that the team leader is the most important motivational determinant.[12]

A *master system architect,* with assistance from specialized system architects as needed, designs the system portion of the *operating* concept. She receives counsel from the chief information officer, the project owners, the project managers (if assigned), and various groups and committees. *After* the operating concept is formulated and approved, system architects, *under leadership of project owners*, create and structure *project* conceptual designs which will, upon approval, serve as the basis for project execution led by project managers who also will report to the project owners.

The Transformational Project Paradigm (TPP) forms a logical process for adapting the operating concept and related systems to meet new requirements when a significant change or opportunity occurs in the marketplace, or as more detail becomes known during the formulation of project concepts. Thus, a company can have a way to ensure that revisions are implemented effectively because the management controls and procedures will already be in place.

Figure 1.4 depicts a high-level operating concept example of internal financial reporting for a global corporation. The transformed flow offers a superior concept made possible by advanced information technology. Data is shared through networking and data storage instead of summarizing and passing it upward in the organization. Fewer steps make the

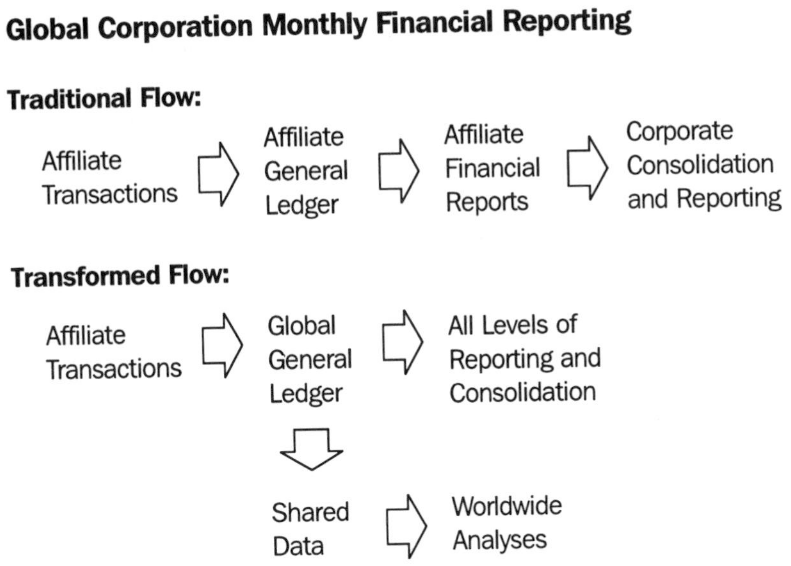

Global Corporation Monthly Financial Reporting

Traditional Flow:

Affiliate Transactions ⇨ Affiliate General Ledger ⇨ Affiliate Financial Reports ⇨ Corporate Consolidation and Reporting

Transformed Flow:

Affiliate Transactions ⇨ Global General Ledger ⇨ All Levels of Reporting and Consolidation

⇩

Shared Data ⇨ Worldwide Analyses

Figure 1.4 High-Level Operating Concept Example

---

transformed flow faster than the traditional one, and the same transaction data is available for query and analysis by all parties.

Note that the transformed flow in Figure 1.4 represents discontinuous change. No amount of incremental change in the traditional flow would create the same result. Discontinuous change demands that concept formulation, *how the system can operate,* must precede user requirements, *what the system must produce.*

The transformed flow must be tested against user requirements, such as tie-ins with accounts payable, specialized local reporting, and security control, before proceeding with proposal work. Constructive analysis work performed through requirements testing is essential to achieve a workable concept.

Changing to the transformed flow makes final affiliate results available to upper levels of corporate management at the same time that the results are seen by affiliate managers and controllers. This major change in the reporting procedure might not generate enthusiasm at the affiliate level, even though it can be argued that accounting data belongs to the corporation, not to the affiliate. Jack Welch said that one of the big lessons he learned from running General Electric was that change has no constituency. People like the status quo—the way it is. He added in retrospect that he was too cautious and timid and had wanted too many constituencies on board.[13]

Project Concepts

The TPP initiative leader assigns a project owner from the user areas for each project after the master system architect has identified the general scopes of projects within the operating concept. A TPP initiative usually has two or more project owners; one project owner may have more than one project. Each project owner is the person in charge, reporting directly to the *initiative leader* with respect to the project.

The TPP initiative leader and project owner develop business objectives, a subset of the TPP initiative goals and objectives, to be achieved through project concept and execution work led by the system architect and project manager. Project concepts divide the work into manageable segments that can be developed and implemented. Subject to project owner review and approval, the system architect:

- sets the specific project scope
- drafts the conceptual design
- compares user requirements against the design
- performs a development alternatives study
- prepares a conceptual design document
- prepares a project proposal
- upon approval, turns the design over to the assigned project manager.

The system architect is then free to begin work on his next assignment while the project manager proceeds with project execution work under the guidance of the project owner. The entire process from TPP initiative

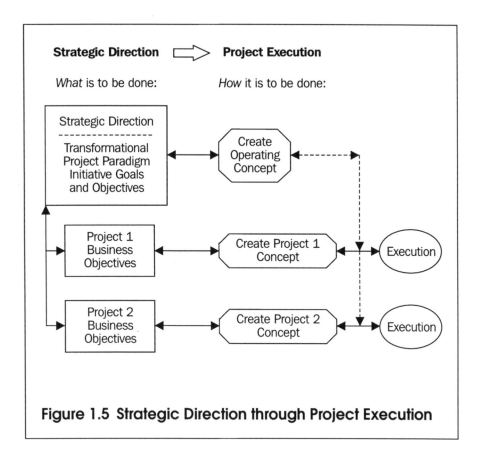

Figure 1.5 Strategic Direction through Project Execution

definition through the operating concept to multiple project concepts and executions has appropriate beginning-to-end accountability, a topic that will be amplified in Chapter 4.

The TPP initiative leader and project owners also are responsible for related, non-system portions of the operating and project concepts, for example, effects on personnel, changes in physical product flow and inventories, and revisions to facilities. (Changes other than the effects on personnel are outside the scope of this book.)

The chart in Figure 1.5 displays how project execution is tied to the strategic direction, or game plan. Note that the TPP initiative goals and objectives, which are part of the strategic direction, interact directly with the concept of how the work can be done—the *operating concept*. Project business objectives and project concepts separate the TPP initiative objectives and operating concept into manageable parts.

The bi-directional arrows indicate that this is a dynamic model. Ideas, issues, and constraints flow in both directions. Systems work is a learning experience for all concerned. Early conceptual definition gives TPP initiative leaders, project owners, and the personnel department lead time to work with user managers and staff members who will be affected by system deployment. More details become known as work proceeds.

Conceptual Change Examples

Although Sam Walton's operating and customer service breakthroughs at Wal-Mart occurred long before definition of the TPP, his visionary top-level concept for Wal-Mart that supported its strategic direction of serving customers with low-cost, high-quality goods is an excellent example of conceptual change.

His vision turned the common slogan *customer driven* into reality by persuading manufacturers, wholesalers, retailers, and consumers to see themselves as "parts of a single customer-focused process rather than as participants in a series of transactions."[14] His all-encompassing concept formed the context for development of supporting practices and systems.

Wal-Mart's cross-docking project provides us with an example of a system that was guided by Walton's overall vision of operations. The resulting business practices and system reduce inventories and speed products from manufacturers to consumers.

As reported in the *Harvard Business Review*, Wal-Mart's cross-docking system moves goods continuously from one side of the dock where they are delivered, to the other side of the dock where they are dispatched to stores, avoiding sitting in inventory during the process. The system requires "contact among Wal-Mart's distribution centers, suppliers, and every point of sale in every store to ensure that orders can flow in and be consolidated and executed within a matter of hours."[15] The *Harvard Business Review* article continues:

> To gain the full benefits of cross-docking, Wal-Mart has also had to make fundamental changes in its approach to managerial control. *Traditionally in the retail industry, decisions about merchandising, pricing, and promotions have been highly centralized and made at the corporate level.* Cross-docking, however, turns this command-and-control logic on its head. Instead of the retailer pushing products into the system, customers "pull" products when and where they need them. *This approach places a premium on frequent, informal cooperation among stores, distribution centers, and suppliers—with far less centralized control.*[16] (emphasis added)

In contrast, other wholesalers and retailers, especially in the packaged-goods industry, were busy buying more goods than they could immediately sell to obtain special deal and volume discount prices from the manufacturers, a practice known as trade loading. Because of this practice, $75 billion to $100 billion in nonperishable grocery products sat in the pipeline at any one time in 1992, which added some $20 billion in cost to the $400 billion that Americans spent on groceries.[17]

Caterpillar provides us with an example of how accountability affects results being achieved through information technology deployment. The company changed from a functional organization (marketing, manufacturing, and so on) to business units (tractors, engines) prior to harvesting significant benefits from information technology. Caterpillar assigned business unit managers profit and loss responsibility, which prompted those managers to look more closely at information technology capabilities. Some of the improvements in information supplied to business unit managers included input to important decisions on design alternatives for their various products, sales focus, and supplier performance. Caterpillar also extended information technology capabilities to its customers to make them more productive, which should lead to higher profits for all parties in the future. As a result, due in part to improved information technology deployment, Caterpillar invests less and gets better results in customer satisfaction, improved market share with 27 percent higher sales, and 29 percent fewer employees than the company had twelve years ago.[18]

Although the two examples start at different points—Wal-Mart with a top-level concept and Caterpillar with restructured business units—they achieve information technology results through two fundamental principles: workable, efficient concepts that address customer desires and the ability to execute projects to bring the concepts into reality.

The Importance of Creative, Conceptual Thinking

The ability to conceive and implement a Transformational Project Paradigm (TPP) initiative successfully through superior operating and project concepts followed by sound project execution is a key factor in the competitive business environment. Opportunities to solve problems and achieve competitive advantage affirm the crucial need for conceptual thinking, especially now that we have a powerful avenue of implementation—advanced information technology.

Robert Katz, a noted professor and early business leader, described in the 1950s the key importance of conceptual thinking skill for executives that still holds true:

> Because a company's overall success is dependent on its executives' conceptual skill in establishing and carrying out policy decisions, this skill is the unifying, coordinating ingredient of the administrative process, and of undeniable overall importance.[19]

The conceptual approach, when implemented through transformational projects, can produce sweeping improvements in the way work is accomplished, provided that the strategic direction is defined correctly for the company. If the direction is not correct for the company in the marketplace, even a well conceived and executed TPP initiative will have little impact.

Results from the best conceptual thinkers in the world are fruitless if the problem is not stated correctly. Peter Drucker warns against coming up with the "right answer to the wrong problem. ... And that, as all decision-makers learn, is the most dangerous course," leading to the irretrievably wrong decision.[20] Although this is a well-known fact, it is deceptively easy to think that one is working on the right problem—indeed to persuade the entire management team that it is so—and yet be completely wrong.

Why Substitutes for Creative, Conceptual Thinking Can Fail

Conceptual thinking in the systems arena demands the ability to visualize relationships between technical components and business practices. Nothing can take the place of applied creative, conceptual thinking at all company levels.

Relying on extensive data analysis to locate problems for correction, or using methodologies to guide the investigative process, or waiting for technical advances to solve the problems, are ineffective substitutes. Yet these approaches can be readily selected for systems work when individuals who are involved in decision-making may be more comfortable with the analytical rather than with the creative, conceptual mode of thinking.

The analytical mode of thinking has its appropriate place when used in the form of *constructive analysis* for evaluation of ideas, and for requirements testing of operating and project concepts. It must *follow* the creative, conceptual thinking mode in transformational project work.

Data Analysis

The purpose of analyzing data is to gain an in-depth understanding of an application area before creating a workable operating or project concept. Real understanding, so necessary for successful progress, frequently comes from business facts that might not be detected by documenting the existing process.

Often the first step in a study is to flow chart the existing process, in part to learn how it works, and also to detect opportunities for improvement. This work can become extremely time consuming and can produce a document that limits thinking to focus on *what is* instead *of what should be*. A serious problem can arise when managers assume that the team understands the process when in fact the team has completed only a study assignment in flowchart form. The team can proceed without knowing what it is doing.

Gathering *excessive* data without first defining the purpose can actually hurt a project according to Gerald Nadler and Shozo Hibino, authorities in problem-solving methods.[21] A significant difference exists between performing a current system study and understanding the goals, issues, and possibilities for improvement. Voluminous data analysis studies, like methodology assignments, often focus on performing certain tasks, instead of on gaining a deep understanding of the problems and issues at hand. Project team members can devote time unproductively to assembling, summarizing, and reporting huge amounts of raw data instead of focusing on problem solving and finding new opportunities for improvement.

According to de Bono, information analysis will not yield new ideas because the brain can see only what it is prepared to see (existing patterns).[22] This does not mean that project members do not need to become immersed in the subject area—immersion to gain in-depth understanding is completely different, however, from performing a data analysis assignment to find out all there is to know about the problems.

Methodologies

The role of methodologies is often confusing. Some assert that a project team must have a methodology to approach and solve a problem, while others disagree by saying that senior project team members do not need a methodology and that junior members cannot solve the problem by simply following a structured plan. At the heart of the issue is a pro-methodology belief that solid methods will produce good results. Abraham Zaleznik, internationally renowned in the field of business leadership, disagrees in descriptive language:

> The delusion of the managerial mystique is that solid methods will produce good results. Management's overriding fantasy is that an array of organizational devices and techniques of control will overcome all human frailties. Managers find it difficult to believe the reality that good and bad substantive decisions are directly related to the strengths and weaknesses of the individuals involved.[23]

With respect to systems work, Tom DeMarco and Timothy Lister, experienced information systems consultants and authors, define a methodology as a prescribed, documented way that a class of thought-intensive work ought to be done. They state the benefits that methodology proponents use as standardization, documentary uniformity, managerial control, and state-of-the-art techniques. They observe, however, that the underlying message is that the project people aren't smart enough to do the thinking. They conclude that if project team personnel aren't smart enough to think their way through their work, their work will fail.[24]

The Transformational Project Paradigm (TPP) assumes that people *are smart enough* to do the thinking, *given the opportunity* to develop their individual and team-related skills. Establishment of information systems division home departments, part of the TPP, specifically gives project team members the opportunities to develop their skills. Transformational project success depends on skilled, knowledgeable system architects, project managers, and development team members capable of performing the assignments.

Technical Advances

So much is reported about hardware, software, and communication advances that one might get the impression that business problems are being solved merely by technological progress. In reality, advanced technology provides only the base for transformational projects. *At worst,* it can become an excuse for not addressing real problems because of the belief that the needs will be met simply by waiting. Ironically, *technical progress can delay* operating concept breakthroughs because managers *hope* that a technological answer will appear magically to solve their problems.

A superior operating concept can be successful regardless of whether the supporting application systems run on mainframe, client/server, or network-centric architecture. Senior managers need to weigh the urgency of realizing their strategic direction against the benefits of future technical advances. New technology might make it easier and less costly to achieve the strategic direction at a later date but will never substitute for the informed, conceptual thinking and follow-through that are essential for success in realizing TPP initiative goals and objectives.

In particular, *system architects must be well versed* in technical advances and capabilities in order to prepare conceptual designs utilizing alternative technical approaches. They must be able to evaluate each approach based on thorough, in-depth knowledge gained objectively through study and experience.

The Power of the Conceptual Process

A workable, effective conceptual model at a high level that focuses on the *transformation of work from separate and diverse segments into an interrelated whole* is vital to realizing the full power of the conceptual process. Systems and practices from other sources, when included in the concept formulation phase, must be customized for the actual demands of the specific situation. Creative, conceptual thinking is the fuel that runs the engine of the TPP, driving the entire process.

The power of the conceptual process can *enable* a company to support and sustain growth through realization of its TPP initiatives as part of the company's overall strategic direction. The operating concept aligns the capabilities of advanced information technology with the TPP initiative goals and objectives to establish how business-critical work of the company will be done. Major projects can be linked directly to the TPP initiatives through the operating concept, with management in full control from beginning to end. Development costs in the systems area can serve, as they appropriately should, as an investment in the future.

2

Moving Beyond the Current Situation

In surveying the trends that are most strongly influencing the evolution of information technology in the 1990s, a common theme has emerged from our research efforts, research sponsors, and related literature: *Advances in information technology provide opportunities for dramatically increased connectivity, enabling new forms of interorganizational relationships and enhanced group productivity.*

Stuart E. Madnick, in *The Corporation of the 1990s*

Advanced information technology has brought about the capability for unparalleled, dramatic improvements in productivity, cost control, capital utilization, and customer satisfaction while opening up new opportunities for growth. Global networks now exist that allow simultaneous communication within and among companies worldwide while work proceeds. Software operating systems, database access systems, and application packages evolve with advances in networking, mass storage, and computer speed and capacity. This progress in technology continually brings about new capabilities.

Unfortunately, the projects that make these capabilities a reality for company operations and services have produced mixed results. When important projects are out of control or do not produce intended results, good and talented people can find themselves living chaotic and uncertain lives. Opportunities to develop their skills and move forward in their careers can vanish overnight. Their companies fare no better when money for project work produces little or no appreciable result—only lost time and less money to readdress the problems of inadequate systems.

A 1994 survey of information technology application development projects by The Standish Group, covering 365 respondents representing 8,380 applications across major industry segments and governmental organizations, indicates serious problems in project performance. Based on the sample, companies will achieve full project success only one-eighth of the time. Thirty-one and one-tenth percent will be canceled before completion; 52.7 percent will cost 189 percent of their original estimates with only 61 percent of originally specified requirements; 16.2 percent will be completed on time, on budget, with all features and functions as originally specified. In larger companies of over $500 million revenue per year, the news is even worse—only 9 percent of their projects will be fully successful; projects with overruns will contain only 42 percent of specified requirements.[1]

Cost overruns and write-offs are staggering. Of the more than $250 billion spent each year in the United States on approximately 175,000 projects, the report estimated that in 1995 $81 billion will have been spent on canceled projects, and an additional $59 billion will have been spent on overruns. The survey indicated that one of the major causes for both cost and time overruns is restarts. For every 100 projects that started, there are ninety-four restarts. This does not mean that ninety-four of 100 projects will have one restart; some can have several restarts.

The overall situation does not noticeably improve. Information technology executives in the survey sample are nearly evenly split on whether the situation is getting better or worse compared to five to ten years ago—48 percent say no, and 52 percent say it is the same or better.[2]

The Standish Group finds in its 1996 survey update that 27 percent of the projects will be fully successful as compared to 16.2 percent in 1994. More projects are being canceled, with 40 percent in 1996 compared to 31.1 percent in 1994. The Standish Group explains that information system departments are finally starting to focus on the rigors of project management to improve and are canceling troubled projects more quickly.[3]

Observation about Project Restarts

Unlike a project that has physical end products, such as building construction where visual inspection of the site and study of the architectural drawings present a clear picture of the accomplishments to date, a systems project has little physical evidence of actual progress. Partially completed or untested programs, incomplete documentation, and possible staff changes make a clean restart difficult. Unless the original project manager and team members can restart a project shortly after stoppage, a great deal of time is needed to investigate and retrain. In some cases, it will become necessary to restart the project from the beginning. Thus, money spent to date is likely to produce little, if anything, of value.

Computerworld Findings

Computerworld finds in a 1995 poll of 200 chief operating officers, chief financial officers, and chief executive officers that 52 percent of the respondents say that they are getting their money's worth from information system spending.[4] *Computerworld* observes that the percentage is slightly better than in 1993 and a big improvement from 1989, but that "it's hardly ecstasy." The poll shows executives ranking as a top corporate goal "improving information systems, systems technology and automation" right behind customer sales and satisfaction.[5] Although respondents must have considered project success in their evaluations, the poll is not at project level.

Separately reported in the *Computerworld* article is a quotation from Robert Mittelstaedt, director of executive education at the University of Pennsylvania's Wharton School of Business (United States): "There remains a level of frustration about why things can't happen more rapidly, with more predictable results and costs." *Computerworld* observed that Mittelstaedt should know. In 1994, some 10,000 executives, including 1,000 chief executive officers, were trained by the Philadelphia-based school.[6]

Evaluation

What do the information system results described above tell us? Certainly companies are making progress in systems development. Moreover, setting aside the important restarts cause, the overrun cost reported in the Standish survey could be attributed, at least in part, to the inherent difficulty in estimating systems work, described later in this chapter. If the overruns are measured from original estimates, some might not be real overruns at all, just a result of participants learning more as they progress further in the details, a natural circumstance of systems work. The Transformational Project Paradigm management practices should control restarts and real overruns.

The cost of and fallout from project cancellation is definitely a cause for concern. The $81 billion estimated loss in 1995 is a lot of money. Exxon, the most profitable company in the 1996 Fortune 500, had $7.5 billion in net profit. The top five most profitable companies that year—Exxon, General Electric, Philip Morris, AT&T, and IBM—earned a total of $32.4 billion.[7] It might be argued that many companies do well in spite of information system project cancellations. The fallout on people involved in them is severe, however, with much of it affecting information systems division (ISD) personnel, often unfairly because of weak accountability.

Although the Standish survey does not differentiate cancellations by project size or purpose, abandoned projects researcher Kweku Ewusi-

Mensah, a professor at Loyola Marymount College in Los Angeles (United States), has found in separate research that most canceled projects were systems the companies considered vital to their way of doing business in the Information Age. He states that cancellations are distinctly possible, particularly for large-scale projects, unless proper planning and control tools are used with a commitment to satisfy requirements of the technology and organizational components of the system, together with satisfactory interactions among the three stakeholder groups: information systems staff, end users, and management.[8] Management practices called for by the Transformational Project Paradigm should reduce the number of project cancellations.

The survey and research efforts discussed above do not convey whether superior concepts were employed—concepts that create breakthroughs in growth opportunities, productivity, cost control, asset utilization, and/or customer satisfaction. Projects deemed successful only on the measures of meeting time, cost, and requirements fulfillment might produce little value to the company.

Wasting of critical and costly information systems personnel time from project restarts and cancellations has become especially serious in view of personnel skill shortages and increasing employment costs. The Information Technology Association of America estimates that there are 217,000 vacant core information technology employee (programmer, system analyst, and computer engineer/scientist) positions at 97,733 non-information technology commercial firms in the United States with more than 100 employees. This represents 9 percent of an estimated 2,335,000 core information technology employees in those companies.[9] The United States Department of Labor, Bureau of Labor Statistics, estimates that companies will require more than one million new computer engineers, system analysts, and computer programmers by 2005.[10]

Computerworld's 1997 Annual Salary Survey found that chief information officer total compensation rose by an average of 28 percent from 1996 to 1997. Eleven staff positions reported average increases of 10 percent or more—only five positions received less than a 5 percent increase.[11]

Although *Computerworld* questions the way the Information Technology Association of America expanded the sample to arrive at total vacancies, it agrees that a problem clearly exists:

> Regardless of whether the ITAA's labor shortage numbers paint a true picture, there's one point on which everyone agrees: Companies in nearly every industry are reporting serious difficulty in finding and retaining qualified information systems staff, emphasis on the word "qualified."[12]

Although the Bureau of Labor Statistics is known for its rigorous measurement ability, it obtained its numbers by polling the public and private sectors at a time when the United States economy and the information technology industry have never been stronger. The National Science Foundation concludes in a 1993 study:

> It is not entirely possible, and will probably never be possible, to predict with a high degree of accuracy ... shortages or surpluses of scientists and engineers several years into the future. Limitations on projections are especially severe for demand, since demand is a function of the economic cycle and of global events that are difficult, if not impossible, to predict.[13]

The *Computerworld* first quarter 1998 hiring outlook showed that information technology hiring managers in all areas of the United States plan to increase their staffs in the next quarter. Recruiting times have lengthened, and offers are higher for skilled professionals.[14] It is unclear how long the qualified information systems staff problem will persist. One thing is certain—it is with us now.

Bell Atlantic is an example of a company that has improved abilities of its information systems staff. The company established centers of excellence (home departments) in July 1994 for its Large Business and Information Systems unit within corporate information systems, an applications development and maintenance group of about 250 members. The objective was to build an information technology talent base that provides a solid internal pool of skilled information systems professionals trained in current skills (client/server, object oriented, networking), customer relationship management, and project management. The centers are semipermanent teams of technical specialists, or people trained in a specific information technology skill. Each skill center is a virtual homeroom of information systems personnel who share a high level of proficiency in a specific skill set. By making the change, this Bell Atlantic applications group has improved its ability to meet customer needs while reducing its reliance on contractors.[15] Establishment of ISD home departments is described in Chapter 5.

In addition to developing expertise through home departments, the Transformational Project Paradigm, when customized and detailed, can help management to:

- reduce costly restarts, overruns, and cancellations of crucial projects
- foster superior concepts that maximize value received
- form a supportive context for performance of systems work.

These attributes should assist in recruiting and retaining system architects, project managers, and development team members and in using their talents to maximum advantage.

Practices That Diminish Information Technology Results

Ineffective practices can cause companies to trail in their ability to realize benefits from information technology. Some of the problems are: lack of conceptual tie-in of projects with strategic direction initiatives, out-of-control changes in project scope and requirements, improper use of project estimating, and treating project cost as operating expense in management reporting. Additional issues include: managing projects by user and ISD functions, holding ISDs accountable for *all* information technology projects, lack of reporting ISD team member availability, overreliance on technical solutions, and reorganizing user areas without considering advanced information technology capabilities.

Lack of Conceptual Tie-in of Projects with Strategic Direction Initiatives

The conventional systems development approach calls for user requirements as the next step after setting business unit objectives. Users meet with information systems professionals to describe procedural steps, screens, and reports *without anyone* having a clear understanding of *how the system will work* to meet the business objectives in a technically sound manner (a target solution), and h*ow the project solution* will tie in conceptually with the strategic direction initiative established by senior management.

Projects that proceed without a solid conceptual design suffer major problems. Application package evaluation becomes more risky because the conceptual design basis upon which the package should meet business objectives *does not exist.* Scope and requirements changes can become a nightmare because they cannot be tested for propriety against a conceptual design. No one knows how the system is intended to work overall, so what little conceptual integrity exists initially can dissipate. Project cancellation becomes ever more probable because management, unconvinced that the system will meet the business objectives, loses interest and complains about delays and extra cost.

The Transformational Project Paradigm (TPP) calls for conceptual design work, performed by system architects, to create alternative target solutions. User requirements can be tested against the target solutions to see which solution, with necessary revisions, will best fulfill operating needs. Thus, conceptual integrity is preserved, and the possibility of project cancellation is diminished.

Frederick Brooks contends that conceptual integrity as perceived by the user is the most important factor in ease of use. He makes the following observation that includes his definition of the term:

> A clean, elegant programming product must present to each of its users a coherent mental model of the application, of the strategies for doing the application, and of the user-interface tactics to be used in specifying actions and parameters.[16]

Out-of-Control Changes in Project Scope and Requirements

Scope and requirements are related. Widening the scope broadens the extent of work to be done; adding requirements increases the depth of work to be accomplished in a given area. The Project Management Institute defines scope management as "ensuring that the project does all the work required—and only the work required—to successfully achieve the purpose of the project."[17] Requirements detail the specific items within a work area, for example, the screen layouts needed by collectors in a credit and accounts receïvable operation. The overall collection function including screens, reports, payment performance history, and other requirements comprises the work area, a scope item.

Scope and requirements are subject to change during project work. Management must decide how to evaluate, direct, and control the changes. Changes can come from many sources. Five of the main ones are:

- learning by project participants of the actual detailed needs as requirements and specification work proceeds
- incomplete definition of user requirements; this always is true to an extent despite best efforts
- advice from the development team about requirements that cause problems with complexity, time, or cost relating to the software product
- changes in business practices and responsibilities from external and internal sources
- changes in the marketplace.

Often the decision to make individual changes depends upon the relative level of power between the user and information systems division (ISD) areas. If an ISD makes all of the changes requested by the user without an objective evaluation of their impact, time spans and costs can escalate dramatically. In the worst case, the original system design will no longer hold. If an ISD does not make justified changes, the system, when developed, may not work because it does not meet the actual requirements of the work situation.

The probability of major, unanticipated scope and requirements changes is reduced when a qualified system architect prepares the conceptual design in advance of project approval. Scope and requirements work, at progressively lower levels of detail, can continue throughout project execution within a workable, approved conceptual design.

The TPP establishes the basis *for effective determination of scope, and evaluation of requested scope and requirements changes.* When companies have qualified system architects available to prepare project conceptual designs, the responsibility for recommending *scope boundaries* can be established to rest with the *system architect and project owner* because that task is included within the conceptual design.

The TPP requires that three conditions exist: (1) Accountability for project conceptual design and execution must be vested in one person, the *project owner*; (2) The *system architect or the project manager* must assemble the estimated impact of requested changes in terms of time, cost, and technical feasibility for review by the project owner; and (3) The *project owner* must then assume time and cost accountability for the changes that she authorizes.

Improper Use of Project Estimating

Time and cost overruns are caused in part by the difficulty in preparing accurate estimates at project approval time because exact requirements and program specifications are unknown at the time funding is granted. System architects and project managers find difficulty in arriving at accurate estimates for new projects, even in those companies that keep project history records.

Why is arriving at initial estimates so difficult? Specific requirements and specification work, necessary for accurate estimating, continue throughout the project as development proceeds. The nature of a systems project *prevents* having total requirements and specifications available at the outset because they are an integral part of the project itself.

Research suggests that accuracy of the software estimate depends on the level of refinement of the software's definition. The implication of the research is that the effort needed to refine the estimate is the work of the software project itself: requirements specification, product design, and detailed design. Other research findings show that project estimates fall within a predictable variation at various stages of the project. At initial product concept time there can be a factor-of-sixteen difference between high and low estimates. Later, when requirements are specified, the level of effort still can be known only to within about 50 percent, the time that most companies want their estimates to the dollar for budgeting purposes.[18]

Initial software development estimates often are optimistic because, in addition to lacking detailed support, the person who makes the estimate does so for use in a proposal. People who submit proposals usually believe strongly in the benefits to be achieved through implementation, and thus have a tendency either to overlook or to downplay the risks and potential sources of delay. An unspoken concern of a person who proposes a systems project is the fear that it will not be approved if all possible effects of the variables are spelled out.

Company management at times believes the initial estimate to have more importance in relation to the eventual cost than it possibly can have. This is destructive in two respects. An unwarranted reality is attached to the initial estimate that causes project managers and the development team to be measured against an unrealistic expectation, often resulting in an unfavorable effect on morale. The unrealistic original estimate also causes the project team to pursue its work without budgetary control.

The TPP calls for *reestimating of project cost ranges* by the project manager with input from development team members as milestones are reached. Reestimating promotes accountability and is why *fair* performance measurement of the project team members can actually happen. They will be working against a current budget range that they participated in formulating.

A change to *bottom-up reestimating* from directed completion dates might not be received enthusiastically by executives because the reestimates are likely to be higher than desired. Brad Kiewel, who has over eighteen years of experience in software development and project management, finds that executives cool to the process once they discover they can't impose unrealistic product development schedules.[19]

Project owners need realistic estimate ranges from project managers in order to make informed, reasonable decisions on tradeoffs among cost, schedule, and requirements constraints when indicated. Choices to concentrate on meeting the main requirements, adjust the schedule to accommodate unforeseen but important needs, and restrict use of more expensive resources are examples of decisions available to the owners.

Treating Project Cost as Operating Expense in Management Reporting

Companies that treat information systems project cost as an operating expense for management reporting purposes face two negative choices in attempting to solve the estimating problem. If periodic reestimates are created at appropriate times during the project for control purposes, the annual budget numbers will be affected. If the annual budget numbers are kept intact, the project team will not have realistic budget control over their activities.

The Transformational Project Paradigm (TPP) approach provides for project cost to be treated as a *capital budget item in management reporting* starting at the time that the operating concept proposal is approved, regardless of whether TPP project expense is classified as capital or operating for financial and tax reporting purposes. This treatment allows annual operating budgets to remain intact while providing for periodic reestimates for project control purposes. Project cost reestimates should follow company approval policy, including the decision process to continue or discontinue the project. Capital treatment of project cost in management reporting produces three significant advantages: (1) Annual budgets remain intact maintaining control over recurring costs; (2) Realistic budget control is maintained during the length of the projects; and (3) Capital budget reports provide multiyear project period reporting, a contrast with annual periods for operating budgets.

Project budgeting responsibility is placed with *the project owner,* the person who exerts project control from the beginning of conceptual design through final cutover. The system architect and project manager prepare the actual time and cost estimates along with technical feasibility considerations for review and approval by the project owner.

Managing Projects by User and Information Systems Division Functions

A continuing interplay of user requirements and technical development issues exists throughout the life of the project. An information systems project is different from other projects that cross departmental boundaries because requirements definition, although appropriately completed near the outset, actually continues throughout the life of the project. As Donald Gause and Gerald Weinberg, system design consultants and lecturers, observe, "The requirements *phase* ends with agreement, but the requirements *work* never ends until the product is finished."[20]

As the project progresses, more becomes known about user needs and technical considerations that cause changes in project scope and requirements. Even though some believe that requirements can be defined in sufficient detail prior to the start of development, and remain fixed if users devote enough time, energy, and intelligence to the activity, this simply is not the case.

Attempts to define user requirements for handoff to information systems divisions (ISDs) under separate accountability can cause conflict and extra cost. Users can aggressively pursue inclusion of lengthy requirements in the system definition. Information systems professionals, who recall other system projects where they have worked hard to fulfill requirements that were never used, take these strong statements with the proverbial grain of salt and think, "How many of these do they really need?"

At the other extreme, users describe their needs very generally leaving the detailed requirements work to information systems professionals. The technical staff then needs to make assumptions, which are especially subject to change, and often adds features to try to ensure total requirements coverage. Moreover, developers fascinated by new technology are sometimes eager to try out new features, whether or not they are required in their product.[21]

Neither of these attempts at establishing separate user and ISD accountability works well for transformational projects because no one is accountable for objective evaluation and approval of system features. Separation can be very costly. The Standish Group finds in its *Chaos* 1996 study of project failure, covering 360 Fortune 1000 companies, that 45 percent of software features and functions in mainstream business applications are *never used.*[22]

Frederick Brooks states that an underlying problem that severely hinders communication among minds is the lack of physical representation, a given with planning and construction of buildings, roads, and bridges. Such three-dimensional representations are powerful conceptual tools not available in software development.[23]

What does the inability to set handoff points mean in respect to accountability? Since it is impossible to split project accountability *fairly* between user departments and ISDs for transformational projects, when the split is attempted, the senior general manager to whom the departmental managers ultimately report becomes the person responsible for success or failure of the project. Russell Archibald, an internationally recognized authority in project management, notes that every project must have an owner/sponsor in the figure of one senior manager within the owner organization. Without this designation, the general manager— often the chief executive officer—falls heir to the role.[24]

Holding Information Systems Divisions Accountable for *All* Information Technology Projects

In view of The Standish Group project performance survey statistics, it is understandable why business managers are willing to let project success or failure responsibility rest with information systems divisions (ISDs). This "leave it to ISD syndrome" masquerades in many forms; for example: "We are too busy." "We are not technically qualified." "Other work is more important." "We cannot manage a job we do not understand."

When senior general management believes that ISD management is responsible for project problems, action often is taken to change that division's management, much like the action taken with other low-performing units. Indeed, this has been the main tool used in dealing with frustrating information technology performance shortfalls[25] but is likely to be counterproductive.

Knowing that project definition and development are closely intertwined between users and ISD personnel, it is unlikely that senior general management *really knows* the reasons for poor project performance. It is altogether too easy to believe that since the ISD does most of the actual work the ultimate responsibility should lie with it.

A company's ability is *reduced, not increased,* by an ISD management change when the *lack of project owner accountability* is a major underlying problem. The next chief information officer and his management team is likely to be given less time to succeed, which contributes to yet another performance shortfall, again to be replaced by new personnel who, in turn, come under even more pressure to catch up. In this way companies *systematically reduce* their abilities to develop essential systems even as the need for them becomes more important.

The economic livelihoods of the chief information officer and other ISD managers and staff are *unfairly* at stake when they are held accountable for business-critical projects over which they have little control. When high turnover of information systems personnel occurs in a context of frequent reorganization, staff can be easily but unfairly blamed—

with careers damaged and families affected. Misplaced accountability, power plays, and costs in time lost and money spent using the trial and error approach produce frustration and failure all around.

The Transformational Project Paradigm (TPP) establishes accountability for a strategic direction TPP initiative with the TPP *initiative leader* and related project accountability with the *project owners*. To provide the TPP initiative leader and project owners with the capability to create conceptual designs and develop related systems, system architects and project managers, with support from a development team, are assigned to the TPP *initiative leader and project owners* from their home departments in the ISD. By doing this, beginning-to-end accountability is established from the TPP initiative goals and objectives through final cutover of the related systems.

Lack of Reporting Information Systems Division Team Member Availability

Although most ISD organizations have project tracking systems that report individual project progress, chief information officers should receive a report forecasting overall staff loading *by person, skill, and time period* to support informed decisions for acceptance of new initiatives or projects. Russell Archibald recommends producing this type of forecast report by summarizing the plans of all projects planned and under way.[26]

The TPP calls for a comprehensive information systems division (ISD) *project resource report* that forecasts overall staff loading by person, skill, and time period. The ISD project resource report promotes informed decisions by the chief information officer: to accept new initiatives and projects, to manage personnel assignments effectively, and to know how much personnel capacity is either being used or promised. This kind of report can promote effective personnel utilization and reduce significant overcommitments by the chief information officer.

Overreliance on Technical Solutions

Costly recurring disappointments can occur when fascination with a new technology draws management attention away from evaluation of business problems and a planned conceptual approach to their resolution. Nadler and Hibino observe: "Indeed, whenever people simply apply a new technology wholesale, regarding it as *the* solution to their problem, rather than asking first about the fundamental purposes of their productive activity, the so-called solution will tend to do more harm than good."[27]

Bill Gates also warns against attraction to technology before considering how the business should work:

> Instead of rushing out to buy the latest and greatest equipment for every employee or investing in a network, managers in a company of any size should first step back and think about how they'd like their business to work. What are its essential processes and its key databases? Ideally, how should information move?[28]

Concentration on technology can be an outgrowth of the ISD's whole responsibility for project performance. Since system architects and project managers report to technically oriented managers in ISD under this arrangement, they are not required by the reporting relationship to become knowledgeable in business goals, objectives, and user job content. Their inclination is to be expert only in technology. This orientation prompts them to apply technologies to business areas that they may not fully understand.

System architects and project managers working within the dimensions of the TPP report on a project basis to the TPP initiative leader or project owner, as previously stated. They serve as intermediaries between the user community and technical development team members. System architects and project managers must be well versed in business goals, objectives, and user jobs—as they are in technical subjects—to perform this essential communication responsibility.

Reorganizing User Areas Without Considering Advanced Information Technology Capabilities

Historically, user area reorganizations have proceeded without consideration of information technology capabilities because systems have supported processes and functions. Advanced information technology interaction with the strategic direction can bring about sweeping change in the way business is done, superseding existing functions and processes.

Under the TPP, advanced information technology becomes a determinant of how user personnel can be organized to support the operating and project concepts after system implementation. Two situations should be considered. Where no physical products are involved—for example with the banking and insurance industries—the concept of how advanced information technology is deployed determines, in large part, how the work itself can be performed. Thus, reorganization of user departments, if done, should wait until that determination has been made. When physical products are involved, as is the case with a supply chain optimization TPP initiative, the most effective and efficient means of production and transportation, considering advanced information technology capabilities, becomes the major determinant of organization.

The principle of *organizing around the way the work is to be performed* is the common denominator in both cases. The essence of the operating concept is to have senior management concentrate first on the optimum way to meet the goals and objectives of a TPP initiative, instead of focusing on resource reorganization. The TPP calls for reorganizations in connection with TPP initiatives to be performed, if done, *as a consequence of and in coordination with the operating and project concepts.*

The relationship between the Transformational Project Paradigm (TPP) and reorganization will be explored further in Chapter 3.

3

Reorganization as a Change Lever

> ... a core dilemma for executives and leaders is how to maintain stability in their organizations and, at the same time, provide creative adaptation to outside forces; stimulate innovation; and change assumptions, technology, working methods, roles, and relationships, and the culture of the organization itself.
>
> Richard Beckard and Reuben T. Harris, *Organizational Transitions*

For many years senior management has placed emphasis on reorganization through hierarchies and structures to improve productivity and to achieve better alignment with corporate objectives. Indeed, this approach has been effective in many circumstances to achieve improvements in results, although the changes do little to enhance the way the work itself is performed. As observed by Jon Katzenbach and Douglas Smith of the McKinsey Group: "For literally hundreds of years hierarchies and structures have helped organizations create wealth through focusing, dividing up, and setting useful boundaries around jobs, tasks, and responsibilities."[1]

To illustrate how often reorganization has been used as a change lever, a 1994 national survey of 350 executives across fourteen industries by Arthur D. Little on managing organizational change showed that new organization structure and new strategic direction choice actions (both at 23 percent) led as the two most significant changes. Business process redesign ranked fifth with 8 percent while new system application development was not even mentioned.

The same survey reported that although a solid majority of the executives expressed confidence about their companies' success when it came to reducing overhead, increasing customer satisfaction—and even improving profitability and shareholder value—the same respondents were strikingly less confident about their ultimate abilities to empower workers and to enhance employee satisfaction. Arthur D. Little questions how organizations can expect to accomplish only some of these challenges without also succeeding at the others.[2]

Today's global, fast-moving business environment requires a more powerful means of creating wealth than through reorganization: advanced information technology deployment using superior concepts. Instead of focusing and dividing work to achieve manageability and control, technology opens new and broader possibilities by cutting across all boundaries. People can collaborate electronically from distant locations as if they were at the same site. Visibility of records can be achieved through worldwide networks, and routine control of workflow can be monitored through a system instead of through management supervision.

With the advent of high capacity data communications, designers located in different parts of the world can, for example, work together to create aircraft and automotive digital models. Far-flung consultants can prepare proposals and have them reviewed by managers online in a fraction of the time and cost it would have taken to draw the group together to perform the task. For the first time, companies can assign the most qualified people to a task regardless of location.

Advanced Information Technology and Empowerment

Jessica Lipnack and Jeffrey Stamps, networking consultants and authors, state that research since the late 1940s has shown that the pace of change in a business' environment greatly affects how its organization operates. Typically, these studies place organizations along a yardstick that has *mechanistic* types at one end and *organic* types at the other. Lipnack and Stamps define these two organizational modes as follows:

■ Authority runs *mechanistic* organizations, with a strict chain commanding people who perform highly specialized jobs. Superiors pass instructions, decisions, and orders down to subordinates.

■ *Organic* organizations, while they do have authority structures, do not depend on them. Instead, people enjoy rich communication links that enable them to tolerate less clearly defined jobs. With consultation and broad access to information, self-control rather than top-down command is the *modus operandi*.[3]

Mechanistic and organic forms may have the same organizational chart on paper. The difference between the two is the level at which decisions are made. Under the mechanistic form, managers make the decisions that they give to subordinates for implementation. In the organic mode, work groups are empowered to make decisions relating to the normal flow of business, while policy, directional, and funding authority decisions are reserved for management.

Raymond Miles, professor emeritus and former dean of the University of California (UC) Berkeley Haas School of Business (United States), and Charles Snow, professor of business administration at Pennsylvania State University (United States), set forth the level of empowerment visualized in the emerging human investment philosophy for network organizations:

capability ... [the philosophy] focuses not so much on current capabilities as on the potential of organization members to develop broad technical and self-governance skills, that is, the capability to grow new competencies to meet tomorrow's needs. This belief in essentially unlimited human potential encourages continuous investment in the company's human assets as the means of maintaining organizational effectiveness in a constantly changing environment. ...

trustworthiness ... [the model attributes] trustworthiness not only to members of the immediate firm but to upstream and downstream partners across broader networks as well. Again, the belief that people inside and outside the network firm will meet expectations and respond creatively implies that managers can afford to make investments and take risks in the interest of continuing organizational adaptation and improvement.[4]

Miles is also director of the new UC Berkeley Center for Organizational and Human Resource Effectiveness (COHRE).[5]

Advanced information technology supports the organic form of work performance and the human investment philosophy because it provides the data and communication means for collaboration. Transformational project deployment brings this capability to business-critical areas, opening opportunities for significant advances in company operations and services.

Natural Scope

No longer do hierarchies and structures define the scope of work performance in operational and service areas—*systems do*. Broad capabilities of advanced information technology can determine the scope—for it is the *concept* of how systems are deployed to realize strategies that now sets the boundaries. I define interrelated tasks that support a set of goals and objectives as the *natural scope* of a system.

The natural scope can cut across function, process, business unit, geographic, and/or company boundaries leading to significant improvements in productivity. Electronic coordination, in addition to being far faster than other kinds of coordination, can give all participants access to a single data source to eliminate misunderstandings and wasted time lost in finding out the actual status of records. John Rockart and James Short of the MIT Sloan School of Management (United States) argue the importance of information technology in respect to addressing the organizational problem of interdependence:

> information technology provides a new approach to one of management's oldest organizational problems: that of effectively *managing interdependence*. Our fundamental thesis is that a firm's ability to continuously improve the effectiveness of managing interdependence is the critical element in responding to new and oppressing competitive forces. Unlike in previous eras, managerial strategies based on optimizing operations *within* functional departments, product lines, or geographical organizations simply will not be adequate in the future.[6]

In the past, the sequence of goals, strategy, organization, people, and measurements had become an accepted decision process for all organizational models whether they were functional, process, business unit, or others. Although every organizational model has its pros and cons, the thought sequence worked well as long as the scope of systems fell within the boundaries of the structures set up by management. That has changed for TPP initiatives where advanced information technology is central. The traditional sequence can apply for non-TPP initiatives where advanced information technology is not considered a vital component.

Reorganization versus Transformational Project Paradigm Initiatives

Reorganization addresses the structure in which work is to be accomplished *without first establishing the conceptual relationship of advanced information technology to the company's strategic direction* focused through Transformational Project Paradigm (TPP) initiatives. Successive reorganizations often take place—*in areas where the potential of advanced information technology is central*—that cause little appreciable change in how work is performed. In fact, reorganizations can delay actual improvements in work methods because uncertainties and insecurities about future roles consume employees' attention.

This outdated approach carries with it the implication that managers in charge of their individual units, organized by function or process, will optimize the work within their areas of responsibility and coordinate sufficiently with other managers to reach the business objectives and goals of the strategic direction. The subordination of interdependence between functions or processes to efficiency of the individual unit prevents dramatic improvements within the natural scope of the overall system. As argued by Rockart and Short, managerial strategies based on optimizing operations within units will not be adequate to meet competition in the future.[7]

Transformational project work can proceed without disturbing existing organizations. Since advanced information technology, using the TPP, can determine how the work will be performed, reorganization can be delayed in areas where advanced information technology is central. Reorganization in affected business areas, if done, can be deferred until senior management has clearly in mind, through the formulated operating and project concepts, the way in which the TPP initiative business goals and objectives will be activated and project work has begun.

Advanced information technology, especially networking, is bringing about a change in the traditional approach, which, if capitalized upon, can increase the probability of breakthroughs in business practices. The traditional management thinking sequence must change to a much more powerful decision sequence—choosing how best to deploy technology through superior concepts before determining organizational structure. Making this basic change in approach will give management the opportunity to gain maximum leverage from technology through the TPP.

James Cash, professor of business administration at the Harvard Business School (United States), contends that the impact of information technology on organizational change is vital: "The biggest value of today's tools for storing, processing, and sharing data is the opportunity to transform people's jobs, their reporting relationships, and management controls."[8]

Forms of Reorganization

David Cleland illustrates the traditional sequence of strategic implementation in *Project Management: Strategic Design and Implementation* where he showed systems as the fourth step after strategy—following *structure*, roles, and manager/follower style as the three intervening steps, in that order.[9] That was the accepted sequence before advanced information technology freed work concepts from organizational structures. Today system concepts must interact directly with the strategic game plan to achieve maximum results.

Centralization/Decentralization

Centralization/decentralization is one of the oldest forms of reorganization. It involves reassignment of responsibilities from headquarters to divisions or to other decentralized units, or the reverse. The same work is performed but by different people at another location. Historically, decentralization often was followed in a few years by recentralization, and then a few years later the cycle was reversed.

The deployment of advanced information technology can be a determining factor in what functions to centralize or to decentralize within a company because TPP operating and project concepts determine the way broad-based work can be done to achieve TPP initiative goals and objectives. Senior management may wish to centralize or decentralize certain activities based on the capabilities of advanced information technology. This is a much more effective way of making such decisions because it is based on how best to perform the work rather than where to perform it. The *Harvard Business Review* observes that technology has brought about a third option that can obviate the either/or decision:

> In the past, managers had to choose between a centralized and a decentralized structure. Today there is a third option: technology-driven control systems that support the flexibility and responsiveness of a decentralized organization as well as the integration and control of a centralized organization.[10]

Effective deployment of advanced information technology guided by superior operating and project concepts can facilitate the third option, superseding the need to decide upon centralization/decentralization issues by facilitating cross-boundary operations and services.

Restructuring

Restructuring has many variations. It can, for instance, involve closing underutilized facilities, selling off product lines or divisions, or splitting a large company into separate, smaller companies. Some restructuring initiatives can, in fact, be TPP initiatives; for example, if an operating concept creates efficiencies in the supply chain, certain facilities can become redundant. In cases such as this, restructuring becomes a *result* of the optimal deployment of advanced information technology. If contemplated restructuring applies to the operations of the company, senior management should consider capabilities of advanced information technology as an integral part of its decision process. If advanced information technology can affect the extent of potential restructuring, a Transformational Project Paradigm (TPP) initiative instead of a non-TPP initiative might be warranted.

Downsizing

Downsizing, using our definition, is reducing staff without shifting the organization. Although this action may, and usually does, take place in connection with restructuring and reengineering, it can occur on its own. The theory behind it is that the work can be accomplished with fewer levels of management and a reduced number of employees.

Effects on personnel are reported as being distributed bimodally—top executives are rewarded handsomely while middle management, clerical, and production workers are worse off.[11] Unless the company is in an overstaffed condition before downsizing, the reduced work force will have less time to devote to work method improvements, so staff costs often will rise if business picks up or when the affected people reach the limit of their capacities.

The Wall Street Journal reports on a problem of "corporate anorexia" that comes from excessive downsizing:

> After nearly a decade of frantic cost-cutting, the downside of downsizing is beginning to take its toll: Decimated sales staffs turn in lousy numbers. "Survivors syndrome" takes hold, and overburdened staffers just go through the motions of working. New-product ideas languish. Risk-taking dwindles because the culture of cost-cutting emphasizes the certainties of cutting costs over the uncertainties—and expense—of trying something new.[12]

Running lean and mean can do little except maintain the existing way of doing things. The lack of available staff time to devote to system improvements to reduce workload and to support growth might affect a company's ability to compete. If downsizing is done before the system projects, the user staff might not have enough time to spend on system definition and personal training to get its required participation under way.

If senior management plans to downsize areas where advanced information technology is a significant factor in work performance, the downsizing initiative should be converted to a TPP initiative to obtain the maximum permanent improvement in productivity through implementation of a superior operating concept. Higher productivity and increased visibility of information made possible through effective deployment of advanced information technology can reduce the number of management levels required while increasing employee productivity. Instead of an overworked and burned-out staff, well-trained and prepared employees should be able to handle the increased workload if the required systems are conceptually sound and implemented properly, including adequate training.

Reengineering

David Garvin, a professor at the Harvard Business School (United States) who has focused his research on the general manager's role in process-oriented organizations, argues that although reengineering has provided managers with a powerful means of reshaping individual processes so that they serve existing categories of customers more efficiently and has helped managers harness the formidable power of information technology to improve process performance, it is primarily a tool for achieving operational improvements, not total solutions. He raises the question about whether a process should be improved or radically transformed to accommodate strategic requirements.[13] Garvin notes three limitations of reengineering:

> a growing number of managers are discovering that ... reengineering [has] three severe limitations. First, [the technique assumes] that process redesign can be divorced from rethinking business strategy. ... Second, [although] reengineering [is a powerful tool] for redesigning individual business processes, [it often treats] processes as unconnected islands. ... Third ... reengineering efforts typically focus on redesigning business processes and ignore management processes—the ways senior managers make, communicate, implement, monitor, and adjust decisions, and measure and compensate performance.[14]

The reengineering approach has an underlying assumption that employees within separate functions cannot coordinate their activities to serve the customer. The real problem, however, can be the lack of effective cross-boundary systems that, if present, can provide customer focus regardless of how the individual employees are organized. Proper deployment of advanced information technology can dramatically improve cross-boundary communication and coordination without reorganizing.

It may be that instituting cross-functional systems to enable reengineered process-oriented organizations has either been largely accomplished or is considered less important now in North America. The Computer Sciences Corporation 1997 information systems management issues survey showed that the instituting cross-functional information systems dropped in importance ranking from third to ninth from 1996 to 1997. Implementing business reengineering dropped from tenth to fourteenth, after ranking first in four of the six years from 1990 through 1995.[15]

Personnel Issues

Eight issues of *The Harvard Business Review* among those published from May–June 1977 to May–June 1988 observe that "significant increases in productivity are found when management has free rein to deploy workers in the most flexible manner."[16] Advanced information technology capabilities promote that end by making a broad array of data readily available to all concerned.

No longer is it essential to organize for narrowly defined work efforts. Organization can follow the natural scope of work defined by the best way that advanced information technology can be deployed to reach business objectives. This requires thinking about the TPP operating concept first rather than trying to determine scope of work and organization without the benefit of knowing how advanced information technology can transform the work in question. Employees can find superior concept development an engaging and unifying activity.

Employee Morale

Rather than seeing reorganization as a useful and positive lever for change, employees often see it as a way to extract more work from them without commensurate benefit. The problems in accomplishing the work, which were present before the reorganization, continue to exist but with the added complications of changed relationships and computer systems that were designed for the old organization. Often, reorganizations cause people to work longer hours with additional demands for coordination (meeting) time. Consider the horizontal reorganization experience at Lands' End:

The move brought together people who had different jobs but worked on the same product. For example, it teamed artists, who lay out the catalog pages, with merchants, who buy the products, and with copywriters who penned the descriptions. Before the company had been divided functionally, with, say, artists working alongside artists.

The reorganization caused confusion, and had a troubling side effect: meetings. "I was going to meetings five days a week," says Scott Jacobson, a supervisor in the company's quality-control department. "We spent so much time in meetings that we were getting away from the basic stuff of taking care of business." His normal workweek stretched to 55 hours from 45 hours.[17]

By looking at the need to increase productivity as a visibility issue, improved automated techniques can become a solution path letting all concerned view products on order, catalog pages, and item descriptions. Product pictures and specifications, artwork, and descriptions can be viewed in digital form. Coordination becomes an issue of viewing and updating the material electronically, cutting through the need for many of the meetings. Rather than spend extra time in meetings, or alternatively, lose out on necessary coordination, dedicated staff members can perform their jobs in less time while continuing to build their specialized expertise. This contributes to employee satisfaction.

The TPP allows those who participate in defining target solutions to concentrate on solving the problem at hand—regardless of how they are currently organized. Opening up new avenues in how work can be performed without disruption from reorganization promotes employee growth and career development in addition to bringing benefits to a company's operation. The TPP approach fosters worker empowerment because it opens many possibilities for breakthroughs and continuing improvements.

Retention of Trained, Valuable Staff Members

Retention of well-trained and capable staff members, supported by policies of worker empowerment and employee satisfaction, can mean a great deal in terms of increased productivity and added customer satisfaction. A Bain & Co. study estimated that a decrease in the customer defection rate of 5 percent can boost profits by 25 to 95 percent; the knowledge employees gain over the years becomes critical to keeping customers loyal. Moreover, employees who stay about ten years are three times more productive than when they started work.[18]

A survey of manufacturing executives by the Center for the Study of American Business confirmed the importance of human resources in gaining competitive advantage. In response to a question about people becoming relatively more important in gaining that advantage, 88 percent agreed (48 percent strongly, and 40 percent somewhat). Even more startling, given downsizing initiatives, was the finding that 73 percent of the executives agreed (44 percent strongly, and 29 percent somewhat) that it is more critical to reduce turnover of experienced personnel as compared to five years earlier.[19] Loss of such employees might be one reason why downsizings have shown mixed financial results.

The American Management Association found in a separate survey that 75 percent of the companies that had downsized reported that morale had collapsed. Two-thirds of the respondents said that their companies showed no increase in efficiency and half saw no improvements in profits. Negative impacts were more evident in the multiyear downsizers than for those with just one event.[20]

Alvin and Heidi Toffler, scholars and social thinkers, maintain that "Third Wave" Information Age technologies "require diverse and continually evolving skills—which means that workers become less and less interchangeable."[21] Learning curves are becoming longer and more frequent as staff members expand their knowledge and skills to understand and perform additional tasks using the required technology. Even if compassionate employee management principles were set to one side, the reality of business today demands recognition of the need to develop and retain experienced, knowledgeable employees.

Productivity, Capital Utilization, and Customer Satisfaction

In respect to the potential for productivity improvement, research by George Stalk and Thomas Hout of The Boston Consulting Group (United States) showed that organizations are receiving value for only 0.05 to 5 percent of the time that most products and many services are in value delivery systems of their companies. The potential for improvement from successful deployment of advanced information technology is astounding—an increase from 5 to 10 percent value-added time produces a 100 percent rise in time productivity.[22] Where no physical goods are involved, as is the case with clerical and knowledge work, workload leveling combined with the proper use of advanced information technology can create huge improvements in value-added time.

Advanced information technology can replace capital when production of physical goods is involved. For example, General Electric's Transportation Systems Division turned its inventory twelve times faster and saved an acre of warehouse space in the building of locomotives when it began using advanced information processing and communications to link up with suppliers.[23]

By becoming more flexible in receiving and grouping orders and developing an integrated manufacturing system, Mead Corporation is now able to guarantee the same delivery performance for its Fine-Paper Division, with only 20 percent of the inventory previously needed, by delivering better information to the people who make the decisions. With new networking technology, officials at Mead predict an era of global economies of scale.[24]

Meeting the Challenge

Advanced information technology has changed the equation: rather than being bound by the traditional work delegation sequence of scope, organization, job definition, and manager accountability enabled by information technology; advanced information technology itself has become a *determining factor* in how a company can realize its strategic direction through TPP initiatives. Consequently, successful deployment of advanced information technology offers an exceptional opportunity to increase customer satisfaction, as productivity and capital utilization requirements are addressed.

Continuing to reorganize, instead of conceiving and developing transformational systems, can risk the viability of a company. Changing to this new approach is a crucial decision. By looking first at the opportunities that advanced information technology can bring to a company, senior management can achieve breakthroughs in growth opportunities, productivity, cost control, asset utilization, and customer satisfaction that simply cannot be achieved through any form of reorganization.

Part II

Supportive Management Practices

4

Beginning-to-End Accountability

Accountability means that people are answerable for their decisions and actions. To the extent that accountability is diffuse, we
can expect to find things falling through the cracks, inadequate
levels of follow-through, and finger pointing when things go wrong.
J. Davidson Frame, *The New Project Management*

ood management requires accountability for Transformational Project
Paradigm (TPP) initiatives, as for any other business activity, because
accountability for results increases the likelihood of success. The
ability to delegate accountability properly for each stage of the process is
crucial to senior management's responsibility for overall results from the
deployment of advanced information technology. Yet in many companies
one is hard pressed to find *who* is accountable for conceiving superior
operating and project concepts, or for managing development projects.

General agreement exists that advanced information technology must
be applied across organizational unit boundaries to reach its potential
benefits. As noted in Chapter 3, Rockart and Short argue that "information technology provides a new approach to one of management's oldest

organizational problems: that of effectively *managing interdependence.*[1] How to establish accountability across boundaries for transformational project work to bring this interdependence into being becomes a crucial issue.

To make accountability effective, managers will need to make appropriate initial decisions and continue to stay engaged with the process as concepts are formulated and systems are developed. Hogbin and Thomas cite the need to stay involved by stating: "Good decisions and successful projects depend on the understanding and participation of those affected by the decision process."[2] Senior managers must participate *throughout* the entire cycle to assure that desired results are achieved because new developments and the interdependence of organizational units necessitate continuing review and decision-making.

Political considerations can have an unpredictable influence on decision-making. When they are known and incorporated into the accountability assignments from the outset, unexpected political battles can be averted. Hogbin and Thomas comment on the universal nature of political factors and the need for their acceptance by the implementors:

> Political considerations in decision-making are universal. Even technical decisions can reflect the personal preferences, ambitions and concerns of those involved. Within limits, this is not wrong provided that the objectives, as much as the means, of the implementation are clearly defined and accepted by the implementors as their personal responsibility.[3]

Although the TPP initiative leader and project owners should allow for personal preferences, they cannot permit them to affect alignment of the operating and project concepts with the initiative goals and objectives.

Empowerment, Accountability, and Integrity

To achieve a collaborative, team-based organization, Edward Marshall, a change management consultant, states "we must have *empowerment with accountability."* Marshall asserts that the consequences for not holding ourselves accountable can be substantial. He says that if we are "out of integrity," sooner or later it will catch up with us in our work relationships.[4]

Single accountability in the minds of some is associated with the old *command and control* management method. It should not be. Accountability is just as important as ever in today's team-oriented work. There is an important difference, however. Accountability belongs to every member of the team, not just to the managers. David Cleland describes the overall requirement:

> Whatever the team's objectives and goals, its culture should establish clear and understandable performance standards that make leaders and team members accountable for their work. Ambiguities in authority, responsibility, and accountability damage morale, allow things to fall between the cracks and allow political solutions to replace reasoned business solutions. Final accountability is a fundamental principle of sound enterprise management and must be designed into the team management philosophy.[5]

The TPP offers a structure where empowerment with accountability can be established *fairly* for all involved. Participants throughout the entire cycle—senior managers, TPP initiative leaders, project owners, system architects, project managers, and development team members—must be willing to hold themselves accountable, which means taking *full responsibility* for the effects of their actions. *Fairness* makes accountability work.

Self-defensive actions can result from viewing accountability as a way to associate potential problems with a person, hoping that this will motivate that person to avoid trouble. Although accountability is necessary as a fail-safe action, its real benefit comes from the personal commitment and alignment with TPP initiative goals and objectives it can produce. At its best, accountability promotes creative solutions to issues and problems that arise during transformational project work. When established *fairly and logically,* accountability becomes a *force* for progress, not simply a *defense* against failure.

A management reporting system that shows project cost and schedule performance, forecasts personnel loading, and describes issues and problems is essential to support beginning-to-end accountability from the TPP initiative definition through final cutover of the related systems. The management reporting system will be discussed in Chapter 6.

Nature of Systems Work and Accountability

Under the TPP, the nature of systems work becomes the frame of reference for accountability assignment. Systems work has four characteristics that demand single accountability for a TPP initiative:

1. Operating and project concepts, by illustrating how TPP initiative goals and objectives can be achieved, serve as a crucial link to project execution.

2. Systems work is interrelated and interconnected horizontally across user and information systems division (ISD) organizational units.

3. Requirements are subject to clarification and change throughout the life of the overall project and its subprojects from initiation of project concept work through final cutover.

4. Software invisibility[6] is part of the nature of systems work.

As a result of these characteristics, systems work is an *undividable process* from TPP initiative definition through cutover of the final related system. An attempt to divide accountability for systems work between user and ISD units *impedes* the ability of a TPP initiative leader and project owner to maintain control.

Subprojects formed by the project manager within the overall project even relate to each other. Sequential implementation of subprojects can involve changes to previously implemented subprojects for workability purposes or to fulfill the objectives of the overall project concept. *Dividing of accountability* for the overall TPP initiative and related projects or subprojects sets up barriers to cross-boundary, lateral communication among participants, which can lead to delays and even failure to achieve expected results *with no one held accountable.* Guidelines for managing operating and project concept creation and project execution are contained in Chapters 7 and 8.

Operating and Project Concepts

Aligning the information systems area with a company's strategic direction has been a long-standing problem as noted by the Computer Sciences Corporation survey referenced in Chapter 1.[7] Operating and project concepts link the strategic direction *what* with *how* it will be deployed through transformational projects. The Transformational Project Paradigm, by calling for beginning-to-end accountability throughout the process, ties together planning and implementation.

Interconnections

Systems must mirror the flow of goods and transactions. This forces system design to work across function, process, business unit, geographic, and even company boundaries to accomplish project objectives. For example, a product cycle starts with raw materials obtained from suppliers and ends with finished products shipped to customers, a process that involves many organizational units.

An electronic connection is much more demanding, in terms of specific definitions and controls, than manually passing information from one unit to another. Furthermore, cross-boundary electronic systems can change the nature of the responsibilities among organizational units which adds political considerations to the job of defining the interfaces and processing needed to make the system work. Cooperation by all user and ISD unit managers working within the scope of the project is essential to success.

Requirements Clarification and Change

Requirements may need to be changed at any point throughout the cycle because they have been found infeasible or too costly. System development involves a feedback loop to requirements from the ISD as well as a feed forward loop from the users. Thus, software development is a two-way iterative process that requires close communication and understanding among all parties. Despite the noblest of efforts, user and technical participants cannot anticipate everything.

Additional learning gained by the users and project team members during system development forces some requirements changes and generates belief in justification for others. Michael Cusumano, an Massachusetts Institute of Technology Sloan School (United States) professor and co-author of *Microsoft Secrets,* has found that a growing number of companies in software and other industries now follow a process that iterates among design, building components, and testing. Microsoft's experience suggests that the feature set in a specification document may change by 30 percent or more.[8]

Even if users and technical participants could be clairvoyant in their definition of requirements and constraints, the specification level of detail issue would remain. Unlike architectural drawings for a physical creation, neither a system nor a program specification can ever contain all of the detail necessary to proceed independently because of the myriad of conditions that must be addressed through performance of the work itself. Specification to that level of detail would be tantamount to developing the system. This situation demands effective communication among all participants as work proceeds.

Software Invisibility

Frederick Brooks discusses the issue of software invisibility:

> Software is invisible and unvisualizable. Geometric abstractions are powerful tools. The floor plan of a building helps both architect and

client evaluate spaces, traffic flows, views. Contradictions and omissions become obvious. ...

In spite of progress in restricting and simplifying the structures of software, they remain inherently unvisualizable, and thus do not permit the mind to use of some of its most powerful conceptual tools [three-dimensional representations]. This lack not only impedes the process of design within one mind, it severely hinders communication among minds.[9]

System definition and development require creative, conceptual thought that defies physical representation. An architectural drawing with supporting documents for a building gives the contractor the totality of what needs to be done in terms of design, measurements, and materials. A physical creation, such as a building, comes from the mind of an architect but can be represented in three-dimensional form. A contractor can see exactly what needs to be done, which minimizes the need for his understanding of what the architectural vision is—a mental creation of the building.

Completed architectural drawings for the building facilitate a clean handoff to the contractor, making separate accountability feasible for the architectural work and for the actual construction. Questions that the contractor might have of the architect can be answered by reference to an existing portion of the drawings, or by added information from the architect referring to physical components. A key implication of a physical creation, such as a building, is that measurable, three-dimensional data is known *before*, in terms of individual drawings, and *during* construction.

Systems work requires the project owner and project manager to understand the mental creation of the system in the mind of the system architect because systems work *cannot* be represented in three-dimensional form. The building architect can represent his vision in the form of concrete drawings; the system architect cannot escape from the abstract. System flow charts, database content descriptions, user coding structures, and related documentation must be prepared, but nothing exists that will represent the totality of the system architect's mental creation because all documentation is *only a representation of thought*. The thought itself cannot be made concrete. This is what is meant by *software invisibility*, which, by preventing clean handoffs, forces single accountability for the overall Transformational Project Paradigm (TPP) initiative and related projects.

Although prototyping can help communication between information systems division (ISD) and user personnel, the prototype is only *a representation* of what the users will see, not the total system. Sample screens and reports show only the visible aspects of an overall system in digital mock-up form. The actual system must be developed to process real data containing its nuances and exceptions, to work successfully with other system interfaces, to maintain control integrity over the data, and to provide security. Most important, prototypes can only picture requirements—no way exists to prototype a superior concept.

These four considerations—operating and project concepts, interconnections across user and ISD organizational units, the inherent need for requirements clarification and change throughout the project, and software invisibility—demand that *accountability, from TPP initiative goals and objectives through cutover of the last related system*, be placed with a TPP initiative leader.

Accountability Benefits

Given that the entire TPP system cycle from the operating concept through project concepts, requirements, system development, and cutover is a continuum, who should be held accountable for its success or failure? Following normal business practices it should be the person who benefits from a successful result in terms of ability to achieve his unit's objectives. *Project owners*, with delegated accountability from the TPP initiative leader, must therefore assume accountability for the success or failure of their projects from the initial project concepts through final system cutover. In all cases, the TPP initiative leader carries *responsibility* for success or failure of the *overall initiative,* and the project owners assume delegated *accountability* for their *individual projects.* Three major benefits described below should accrue to a company that adopts this policy.

Scope and Requirements Control

Scope and requirements are related, the difference being that widening the scope broadens the extent of work to be done, whereas additional requirements increase the depth of work to be accomplished in a given area. Realizing that a project is a learning process, project owner accountability causes more objective evaluation of requested scope expansion and requirements changes than would split accountabilities. Uncontrolled changes can be a major factor in *project delay, rework, and excessive cost.*

Scheduling

The project manager should be responsible for establishing a reasonable schedule based on estimates from her development team and on personal experience. A national project management survey indicates that a *dictated schedule* is the most frequently cited problem to affect successful management of a project, cited more frequently than project team staffing or poor communications between user and information systems personnel.[10]

Dictated schedules can be a source of project team tension and quality problems by giving the team members a feeling of futility. Such schedules destroy morale because team members feel that they will be blamed unfairly for falling short, regardless of the effort expended and results produced. Since dictated schedules can be a source of project team tension and quality problems, project owner accountability *lessens the likelihood of unrealistic scheduling.*

Budgeting and Cost Control

Project owner accountability places in one person the responsibility for estimating and cost control. Without such accountability, the senior executive to whom the user and ISD principals report becomes responsible for project costs because of the undividable character of the system development process.

Effects of Split Accountability

The chief information officer or another ISD manager cannot be held accountable for the success or failure of a TPP initiative or its related projects because he does not control the operating concept, project concepts, scope, or user requirements.

All four are major determinants of a transformational project's ultimate outcome. If the chief information officer is looked to for TPP initiative and/or project performance accountability by senior management, the senior manager to whom the chief information officer and user department managers ultimately report becomes the project owner and actual project manager by default. According to Russell Archibald, usually the real project manager is found to be the person to whom all those carrying out portions of the project report. It is often a surprise to this manager to discover that he is, in fact, the project manager (and project owner), as he may be several levels up the reporting structure.[11]

Some hold the view that the tension between an information systems division (ISD) and users can be managed by establishing clear policies that specify the user domain, the information technology domain, and senior management's role.[12] Although this assertion is consistent with vertical departmental responsibilities, it does not work for transformational projects, which by their nature cut across organizational boundaries and affect the responsibilities and allocation of work among units within the scope of the TPP initiative. As noted in *The Implementation of Project Management*, clear definition of responsibility and authority of each organizational entity involved in the project usually sounds better in theory than in practice, especially if the project is a complex one.[13]

The notion that all system development problems should be blamed on ISD members because that is the department that performs system development work is simply wrong. When project work fails and reorganizations repeatedly occur with high turnover of ISD personnel, there can be no responsible furthering of system skills for them to take to the next project. Everyone is shortchanged when system skills cannot be developed fully.

Business area project ownership benefits the chief information officer because it lifts from him the overwhelming responsibility for transformational project performance. Gene Bedell, a chief information officer for fifteen years and a chief executive officer for over five years of a company that sells software and services to chief information officers, observes the customer satisfaction problem faced by chief information officers, who are responsible for project performance in addition to infrastructure, standards, development guidelines, and services:

> The CIO's bottom line is customer satisfaction. If users and senior managers aren't happy, the chief information officer is toast.
>
> A CIO might deliver a complex strategically important system on time and within budget to users who fancy they could have done it faster and cheaper, or with a better interface or more functionality. As a result, they're unhappy. Unhappy users wear down even the most supportive senior management as surely as the sea wears away the strongest foundation.[14]

The *lack of beginning-to-end accountability* from senior management through the TPP initiative leaders and project owners *can cause commonly experienced difficulties.* Breakdowns in communications occur. Uncontrolled changes in scope, user requirements, and specifications come from various sources. The responsibility for project problems is placed unfairly between the user and ISD units. Defining and executing projects essential to the company lacks progress, and large expenditures are invested in technology without commensurate return.

Transformational Project Paradigm Management Roles

The Transformational Project Paradigm (TPP) framework is valid for a consolidated company without separate business units, for a company with separate business units, and for other modes of company organization. Unbroken personal accountability from the strategic direction TPP initiative goals and objectives through final cutover of the enabling systems can be maintained regardless of organizational form. The roles described below assume a consolidated company organizational structure and are confined to the main management tasks required for transformational project work, recognizing that broader descriptions of the roles would extend beyond the scope of this book.

Board of Directors

The board of directors must evaluate the degree of importance of advanced information technology to the long-term success of the company. If deemed to be crucial, the board must integrate the effect of advanced information technology into its policy-setting activities. Using the TPP approach, the board reviews, contributes to, and approves the strategic direction of TPP initiative goals and objectives. Also, the board reviews proposals and approves funding and keeps up to date on progress and on current cost estimates. This body establishes and supports the TPP management reporting system that is defined and developed by the chief information officer with counsel from the chief financial officer. Finally, the board asks about any major changes in the system plan that will affect the initiative.

Chief Executive Officer and Senior Management Team

Some of the most imaginative and competitively effective uses of technology have been the "brainchildren" of a chief executive. All the real success stories have been heavily supported by the chief executive officer.[15]

The senior management team, led by the chief executive officer, has responsibility for directing the course of advanced information technology deployment by providing the essential initial direction and continuing guidance as the process unfolds. The chief executive officer and the senior management team should, at the outset, draw on the possibilities and capabilities of advanced information technology to establish the TPP initiative goals and objectives. The chief executive officer-led senior management team has an obligation in today's technological environment to understand the basic nature of the systems development process for use in evaluating progress and for making directional decisions.

The TPP framework requires that the chief executive officer and the senior management team assume accountability, with board approval, for determining goals and objectives that are consistent with advanced information technology capabilities for TPP initiatives; for revising goals and objectives; or for postponing or canceling the initiatives themselves. The chief executive and senior management team set up an environment that supports cross-boundary, decentralized decision-making and development of needed skills. They establish guidelines for job retraining in transferable skills and establish top-level accountability. The team authorizes funds and resources for the TPP initiatives and related projects with board approval as required. It works with the Transformational Project Paradigm initiative leaders, project owners, system architects, and project managers as needed. The chief executive and senior management team assess the relative importance of TPP and non-TPP initiatives if resource conflicts arise and make decisions accordingly. They bear ultimate responsibility for cost and effect.

The chief executive officer, chief operating officer, and chief information officer, in consultation with other senior managers and the board of directors, play key roles in *choosing* the strategic direction TPP initiatives and in *defining* their goals and objectives. In addition, the chief executive or chief operating officer appoints TPP initiative leaders, with concurrence of the chief information officer, who are responsible and accountable along with project owners for the outcome of their respective initiatives. The TPP initiative leader has the authority to delegate accountability for parts of the initiative represented by project business objectives to business managers who serve as project owners under her direction in respect to the initiative. The chief information officer remains the *key counselor* to senior management with respect to the direction and viability of the TPP initiatives throughout the course of all transformational project work.

The crucial importance of line ownership and accountability, starting with the chief executive, was confirmed by a report of ten leading organizations in the deployment of information technology. The study of five private and five governmental organizations was performed by the United States General Accounting Office in 1993–94:

> Line ownership and accountability starts with the chief executive. In every one of the successful organizations we studied, chief executives played a strong leadership role in strategic information management. Once the need to change is established, executives soon realize that getting line managers to work differently means putting them in charge of the change process. Consequently, they move to set clear expectations and reinforce responsibility for information management decisions and results with line executives who deal directly with the customer. Where mission goals require work process innovation and information systems that cut across program or functional lines, *accountability must also be aligned with the decision-making authority necessary to rise above existing stovepipes.*
>
> Increasing line executives' accountability and involvement works because it immediately focuses information management decision-making and systems development activities on measurable mission outcomes of strategic importance.[16] (emphasis added)

The impact that a chief executive can have because of his position in the company is illustrated by an example of successful initiative and project ownership described in the same United States General Accounting Office report on leading organizations. In the early 1980s a private sector organization was confronted with business information systems that could not keep pace with growth. The study describes what the chief executive officer of this organization did through line management ownership to dramatically improve the deployment of information systems:

Although the CEO fully recognized the central importance of information management, the difficulty was that the company's IT unit was unable to work with the business units. IT managers usually gave senior line managers excuses why certain solutions could or should not be developed based on cost and existing capabilities.

This frustrating situation forced a fragmentation of information systems development efforts throughout the organization. Everyone built their own systems because they could not agree on what should be built together. To break the deadlock, the CEO gave a senior line official [initiative leader] responsibility for a major officewide information systems project to develop a "paperless" process. While knowing nothing about information systems, the line official ensured that divisions drove all the major project decisions [division heads became project owners]. He forced these divisions to justify individual projects on net benefits. Information management professionals were made responsible for supporting implementation by functioning as investment counselors and product/service providers. Moreover, throughout the project life cycle, corporate leadership reinforced the new line ownership and facilitated the process of ironing out the wrinkles in the new way of doing business.

When the systems and the new processes went on-line, the pay-off sank in. A customer process that used to involve 55 people and 55 procedural steps was reduced to one person, one phone call, and one step. Improved information management reduced data redundancies, improved communications so that staff throughout the organization could be reorganized around the new process, sped the delivery of data and information to both internal and external customers, and increased data quality. For example, documentation on new service contracts sent out to customers went from 14 days down to 3 days.[17]

To supplement their leadership role, the chief executive and the senior management team can be active participants in supporting *continuing accountability* by asking relevant questions initially and later as directional issues arise:

- How is this going to work?
- Within a range of time, when will it be complete?
- What effect will this project have on our technical infrastructure?
- Do we have or can we obtain people capable of doing the work?
- What are the ramifications after system cutover, for example, cost, flexibility, maintainability, and support?
- What are the risks, and the probability and consequences of each?

Troubling information that is received needs to be researched and, if a problem is confirmed, it must be actively addressed.

Chief Financial Officer

The chief financial officer, as the executive most knowledgeable in fiscal and risk assessment matters, performs the following tasks in executing his role under the Transformational Project Paradigm (TPP). He monitors risk of out-of-control costs and assesses external risks in terms of dollar effect, competition, and changes in technology. He analyzes proposed plans for system projects to assess validity of benefits and expected return. He performs special analyses as requested by the chief executive and advises him on financial implications of what is being done or proposed. He counsels the chief information officer on financial and control aspects of the TPP initiative management reporting system.

Chief Operating Officer and Transformational Project Paradigm Initiative Leader

Companies may have a chief operating officer position; if not, the chief executive assumes responsibility for operations. The chief operating officer and TPP initiative leader roles are discussed together because of their close relationship.

The chief operating officer is the senior management team member responsible for all TPP initiative *operating concepts* and their execution as part of her overall responsibility for optimizing operations of the company. The chief operating officer should know how the company performs its work to meet the business objectives in each application area and have sufficient knowledge in information technology to evaluate alternative concepts that will support the strategic direction. She can assume leadership of individual TPP initiatives or appoint leaders.

The chief operating officer, acting as the TPP initiative leader, or her appointed initiative leader(s), formulates a superior operating concept to support the TPP initiative's goals and objectives and revises the operating concept either to accommodate a change in the strategic direction or to exploit a better technological approach. The leader coordinates groups, committees, and consultants to ensure that all relevant input is received, acknowledged, and evaluated for possible inclusion in the operating concept. She acts as the project owner if those duties are not delegated.

Chief Operating Officer/ Chief Information Officer Coordination

No one in the company has a greater vested interest in operating concepts and their formulation than the chief operating officer. The same applies for the chief information officer with regard to the deployment of advanced information technology. The chief operating officer and the chief information officer need to play major roles, working together from their individual areas of strength. Unless one individual is a master of both areas of expertise, common sense brings us to the realization that the two will best serve the company by working as a team, bringing appointed TPP initiative leaders into the process.

The master system architect appointed by the chief information officer (unless she assumes that role), under the direction and supervision of the TPP initiative leader and the chief information officer, begins work to support the implementation of the TPP initiative by creating the systems portion of the operating concept. The TPP initiative leader should lead overall operating concept formulation work to guide and control the initiative.

Chief Information Officer

Responsibility for infrastructure, standards, development guidelines, and services remains with the chief information officer under the TPP and thus is excluded from TPP initiative leader and project owner authority. These areas, for example, include platforms, networks, operating systems, security, common application packages, software development standards, project milestone review meeting and frequency format, database administration, computer operations, and disaster recovery.

A discussion of infrastructure, standards, development guidelines, and services is outside the scope of this book. Rockart and Short, however, point to the importance of infrastructure in the development and deployment of advanced information technology:

> today's new systems require the development and implementation of a general, and eventually "seamless," information technology infrastructure (computers, telecommunications, software, and data). The challenge to IT management is to provide leadership for this vital set of "roads and highways" in a volatile competitive environment.[18]

Within the guidelines of the TPP, the chief information officer's role includes major responsibilities with assistance from the information systems division (ISD) home department managers. The chief information officer establishes an ISD work environment that fosters applied creativity. He establishes and monitors ISD project team *home departments*. Team members can be reassigned or attend training until another project is ready (to be discussed in Chapter 5). He defines the infrastructure, sets standards, establishes guidelines, and offers services used in system development and in continuing operations, as noted above. He consults with other senior managers about the *impact of technology* on the overall strategic direction, and with the chief operating officer, TPP initiative leaders, project owners, and master system architect on creation of the *operating concept*, or serves as the master system architect if that position is not established.

The chief information officer defines and develops the TPP management reporting system with counsel from the chief financial officer. He advises project owners, system architects, and project managers on project concepts and execution. He ensures that the proper number of qualified personnel—either in-house or contractual—are made available to staff-approved projects. He trains and coaches ISD personnel in advanced system development practices and works with the TPP initiative leaders and project owners to assign and evaluate project team personnel.

Project Owner

The project owner is a senior manager in the user area, accountable for project success or failure, who understands business unit objectives and the work involved to achieve them. The system architect and the project manager report to this person. The project owner informs the Transformational Project Paradigm (TPP) initiative leader regularly on the status of the project. The project owner's responsibilities involve the following roles.

The project owner establishes business objectives, taking advanced information technology capabilities into account, formulates a superior project concept aligned with the operating concept assisted by a system architect, and monitors project execution cost, schedule, and quality. She ensures conformance with infrastructure, standards, and services policies set forth by the chief information officer, and requests variations, if needed, for optimal system implementation. She negotiates exceptions to technical policy with the chief information officer if changes are needed for success of the project. She obtains project approval based on the system architect's proposal, arranges for appropriate involvement of all parties, and makes decisions as needed to advance project progress toward the planned completion date.

The TPP initiative leader receives progress reports, budget reports, and open issues from the project owner. The project owner works with appropriate ISD managers on performance appraisal of the system architect and project manager. She anticipates and arranges, with human resources, job retraining in transferable skill areas for those employees who need reassignment, consistent with company guidelines established by senior management. She assists project team members by encouraging support and evaluating constructive criticism from participants at all levels. She understands design and how the system will work in practice.

She stops work if the project is not proceeding correctly, makes necessary adjustments, and continues.

Project owner accountability places upon one person the responsibility for estimating and cost control. Without such accountability the senior executive to whom the user and ISD principals report becomes responsible for project costs, by default, because the nature of systems work demands single accountability from initiation of the project concept through final cutover.

System Architect

The system architect is a *technically qualified, creative person* who can envision alternative ways to employ advanced technology to fulfill the system portion of the operating and project concepts. He must be willing to research the alternatives and be capable of offering workable, conceptual designs for consideration and approval by the TPP initiative leader, project owners, and the chief information officer.

A master system architect formulates the system aspects of the operating concept with assistance from system architects familiar with operations of separate user areas within the scope of the overall initiative. Brooks states that when multiple system architects are needed, a master system architect must be in charge in order to achieve total conceptual integrity. When one individual cannot do all of the work, each component will have its own architect who must report to the master system architect with regard to his portion of the assignment.[19]

A master system architect must be in charge of the entire design to assure that each project concept, formulated and structured by an individual system architect, will be consistent with the design of the TPP operating concept. Brooks argues: "the most important action is the commissioning of some one mind to be the product's *architect* who is responsible for the conceptual integrity of all aspects of the product perceivable by the user."[20]

All system architects learn the business practices of the application areas in-depth. They look for opportunities to make dramatic improvements through proper use of advanced information technology, and test workability of the ideas against user requirements and technical capabilities. They conceive alternative solutions matching advanced information technology capabilities against the strategic direction and business objectives. To formulate the best system approach to achieve TPP initiative goals and objectives, they work with the TPP initiative leader, the project owners, and the chief information officer. System architects design and document the system portion of the operating concept and the follow-on project concepts, and they evaluate application packages that support the project concepts, including the recommendation for the one that best meets the needs in the proposal. They document findings, prepare proposals, and give presentations as required; adhere to ISD infrastructure, standards, development guidelines, and services policies; and structure the project plans for the individual project concepts upon approval in cooperation with project managers.

The system architect, more than any other TPP participant, performs the crucial role of matching advanced information technology possibilities to the TPP initiative goals and objectives, or to business objectives of related projects. No project, regardless of how well it is managed, can be a success if its conceptual basis is wrong. Under the TPP, the capability to do this technical, conceptual work is fostered by assigning it specifically to system architects.

Special emphasis must be placed on effective communication between technically oriented development team members and business-oriented managers and staff members. To meet this need, system architects and project managers must be able to communicate with participants in business and technical terms, according to their roles. This process promotes success in conceiving and developing technically sound systems that achieve business objectives. Companies that do not attend to this communications intermediary role find that an unproductive situation exists, described by Charles Wang, chairman and chief executive officer of Computer Associates:

> The executives were talking about customers, world-class service, global competition, and return on investment. The information people seemed fixated on platforms, client/server computing, and object orientation. I was stunned. The two parties lacked a basic vocabulary to have a meaningful dialogue.[21]

System architects and project managers must provide this vital bridge for communications among management, users, and the development team.

Project Manager

The project manager leads the development team in making the project concept a reality in terms of a working system. To accomplish this end, she must be technically competent, possess leadership and negotiating skills, and have the ability to effectively manage team members who have different skills and work approaches. The project manager has the negotiating skill to coordinate vendor activity. She has the capacity *to make informed, correct decisions* in guiding the work of the development team toward making the conceptual design a reality.

The Transformational Project Paradigm (TPP) requires appointment of project managers from their information systems division (ISD) project management home departments, who report to the owner on a project basis, and selection of development team members from their ISD development resource pool home department, who report to the project manager. Primary responsibilities of the project manager are to: prepare the original project plan in cooperation with the system architect; assemble a qualified project team from the ISD development resource pool home department, drawing upon outside contractual assistance through the pool if needed; and direct and monitor project execution using modern management methods to ensure that project performance objectives are achieved. The project manager updates the project plan, detailing the next phase, in cooperation with the development team, and maintains effective communication among all parties, making sure that problems are brought to light with recommended solutions. She prepares estimate ranges and progress reports for the project owner and chief information officer and adheres to ISD infrastructure, standards, development guidelines, and services policies.

The flow of project-level responsibilities is shown in Figure 4.1. The bidirectional arrows imply fair placement of accountability. Project team members can identify issues that belong to a management member of the chain. For example, a programmer might find a potential need to expand project scope because of an unforeseen optional interface with another system. This decision belongs either to the project owner or to the TPP initiative leader depending on the impact, as estimated by the project manager.

The TPP offers through accountability a means to identify and reward good performers. A company that achieves the advantages of advanced information technology through successful transformational project implementation should create better job opportunities for company employees. Success through growth and profitability can minimize the trauma of downsizing and cost reduction measures that, in part, might need to be taken by companies that are unable to deploy advanced information technology effectively.

Consultants, Contractors, and Outsourcing

Consultants engaged to assist with operating or project concept formulation need to be retained through the system concepts department, the home department for in-house system architects. Similarly, consultants and contractors engaged to assist with project management and system development need to be retained through the project management and development resource pool home departments, even if much of the work

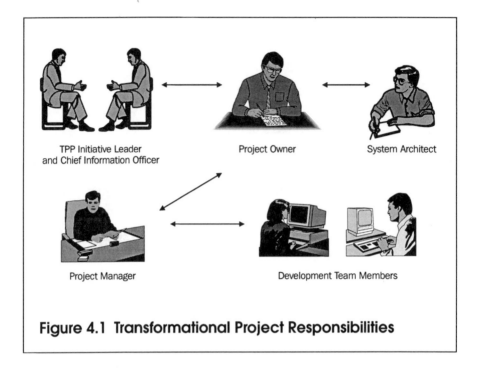

TPP Initiative Leader
and Chief Information Officer

Project Owner

System Architect

Project Manager

Development Team Members

Figure 4.1 Transformational Project Responsibilities

itself is performed at a remote site. This consultant/contractor engagement practice is consistent with the chief information officer being held accountable for furnishing project team personnel, either in-house or through consulting and contracting firms, unless the equivalent of the three information systems division (ISD) home department managers and staff are outsourced. In that case the TPP framework still applies. A discussion of outsourcing pros and cons is beyond the scope of this book; aspects relating to transformational project systems work are considered in Chapter 5.

Consultants and contractors must work *within the beginning-to-end accountability structure* of the TPP framework. Keeping them within this accountability structure promotes ISD participation that enhances the probability of successful system implementation. Danger exists both in adopting outside ideas and practices that might not work for the company, and in feeling that all of a company's practices are superior to others' because of past and current levels of success. Information systems divisions (ISD) must be involved—even if outside consultants are relied upon—in creative formulation of the operating and project concepts for the following two reasons. People do not support what they are not involved in, and information systems divisions can assist in evaluating the workability of the operating and project concepts.

The TPP initiative leader and chief information officer will need to set the expectation that ideas and practices from outside the company will be received and evaluated *objectively* along with ideas and practices that come from within the company.

Sufficient time must be granted to consultants for them to gain knowledge of company practices and to develop the ability to communicate effectively with business managers and staff members. In addition, the chief information officer should become satisfied with the consultants' abilities to communicate with specialized technical personnel and with their performances on prior complex projects.

5

Cross-Boundary Coordination and Information Systems Division Home Departments

The difference between successful companies [in making matrix management work] and the others is the building of an organizational capability to coordinate across units. Almost always the building of the capability meant developing people who could work in teams, exert influence without authority, and feel comfortable in a variety of settings. ...

Matrix success is not based on structure or dotted lines. It is based on the ability to manage conflict, set goals, and jointly evaluate people. These are skills that are built by developing the lateral organization ability. ...

The building of these capabilities is a competitive necessity and, in some cases, it will give a company significant competitive advantage.

Jay R. Galbraith, *Competing with Flexible Lateral Organizations*

The reality of advanced information technology deployment immediately raises cross-boundary issues. All contributors to a transformational project, whether they are in separate functions, processes, business units, or companies, must align their thinking toward the ultimate goals of the Transformational Project Paradigm (TPP) initiative. Although this is an obvious statement, reaching that level of concurrence can be a difficult and demanding experience.

Cross-boundary systems work, by its nature, leads to changes in the allocation of power. A vertical hierarchical organization is usually in place, but the best designed systems cut across boundaries and change the existing allocation of work among the organizational units. Previously decentralized work gets centralized, some tasks vanish, and other, usually more extensive tasks, are created. Formulation and execution of a major advanced information technology project will change the roles of managers and staff members in the various departments and business units because deployment of information technology can empower all management and staff levels with relevant, comprehensive information. Consequently, the need arises to focus on the effect of politics.

Tom DeMarco, an experienced systems consultant and author, contends that software workers are subject to an extra portion of politics, as compared to other fields of endeavor, because of subtle changes in the power structure that accompany a new system. He has formulated a rule and describes accompanying effects which act against optimizing the use of advanced information technology:

Any time a new system is installed or an old one changed substantially, somebody gains and somebody loses power.

Those who build the system and put it into place are acting as agents for this changed power structure.

The parties who stand to lose the most are often the very ones that the system builders have to interact with in order to understand system functionality. These power-losers know that they are essential to the success of the new system. As you might imagine, they are not reluctant to use their temporary strength to force change on the new system, change that will conserve some of their eroding power. Or if that is not possible, they may use their present position destructively to hurt the system-building process and to make it painful for the builders.[1]

Naturally, it can be difficult for a user staff member or manager to contribute knowledge and specify requirements for a system, while fearing that doing so may contribute to loss of personal authority or of one's job. Although such participants may appear to be cooperative in meetings and discussions, they are unlikely to carry through with enthusiasm for and alignment with the project objectives necessary for maximum progress. Recognizing that sweeping change can come with advanced information technology deployment, rumors and misperceptions can create unwarranted fear. Richard Beckard and Reuben Harris, organizational development consultants, state:

Misperception of the implications of a change for one's own future role and responsibilities is a major cause of resistance to change. Resistance can be significantly overcome by providing employees with sufficient information about the end state to provide a more accurate perception about their future role in the organization—and to reassure them that they will indeed have a role to play.[2]

The context of the TPP assumes that the TPP initiative leader and project owners understand and support the operating and project concepts and exert leadership accordingly. A crucial part of this leadership is to manage the effects of the new system implementation on all contributors in the various business areas. The TPP initiative leader and project owners must work cross-boundary with all personnel who will be affected by the planned changes to avoid costly misunderstandings in terms of upsets and work time lost. It is far better to convey these organizational revisions to the people concerned, along with opportunities for transferable job skill training and information about potential new positions, than to try to pick up the pieces on an after-the-fact basis.

Advanced Information Technology System Scope Disregards Boundaries

The natural system scope for advanced information technology concepts is becoming ever broader. Before data communication achieved its far-reaching capabilities, a material requirements system, for instance, only cut across production and purchasing boundaries within a manufacturing company. Now, a comprehensive order entry and production control system can have links to suppliers, customers, and production facilities worldwide.

For example, officials at Mead Corporation predict an era of global economies of scale as noted in Chapter 3. New networking technology allows them to plan to extend their quality and information for decisions system to their mills across the globe to capitalize on the tradeoff between shipping costs and the price of changing a grade of paper in the production process.[3] A high degree of coordination and cooperation among diversified contributors must be attained to make such a broad and complex project feasible.

The Transformational Project Paradigm and Lateral Organization

"The lateral organization model, no matter what its form, is *a mechanism for decentralizing general management decisions*,"[4] as defined by Jay Galbraith, professor of management, IMD (International Institute for Management Development) in Lausanne, Switzerland, and senior research scientist, Center for Effective Organizations, University of

Southern California (United States). Galbraith contends that general management decisions need to be decentralized when:

1. The volume of additional decisions, and the differences among units whose work needs to be coordinated would require more general management capacity, time and energy than is available.

2. Global business strategies require programs or initiatives that cut across vertical hierarchies.[5]

In addition to Galbraith's reasons, sound transformational project decisions require a high degree of technical knowledge supplied by information systems division (ISD) team members that might not be possessed by general managers.

General management integration means drawing together the objectives of separate units into a common end to benefit the company. Accomplishing this can involve suboptimizing individual objectives to arrive at the best overall solution.

The Transformational Project Paradigm (TPP) initiative leader and project owners exercise their integrative roles through business knowledge, line authority, and negotiation with managers outside the scope of their matrix control. System architects and project managers, the other two kinds of integrators, perform their integrative roles through their levels of expertise and reputation. Neither of the latter integrators has authority over user managers or staff although the project manager, of course, has authority in respect to development team direction. The combination of knowledge, expertise, authority, reputation, and negotiation skills is required to make the lateral organizational model work.

The need for the combination of knowledge, expertise, and authority is supported by a study of influence factors from the view of functional managers conducted by Paul Lawrence and Jay Lorsch of the Harvard Business School. They found the following situation in the two high performing organizations of the six that were studied for resolution of interdepartmental conflict:

What the managers in these two organizations were saying was that the integrators were influential because managers valued their knowledge and their expertise. When conflicts arose, all concerned listened to the integrators because they respected their competence. ... The integrators had the assigned authority to help resolve conflict, and their colleagues felt that they knew enough to carry out this assignment.[6]

Lateral organization does not mean the formal reorganization of a hierarchy. Instead, it means that managers and staff in separate units must be able to work together successfully toward a common end, reporting temporarily on a matrix basis to a TPP initiative leader or to a project owner outside their formal chain of command. Transformational project work demands effective cross-boundary direction and coordination led by the TPP initiative leader and project owners.

Matrix management and dual reporting are always required for the relationship between user leadership (TPP initiative leader and project owners) and their ISD managers (system architects and project managers) because no technical staff members work under the administrative authority of the users. This type of management and reporting arrangement also will be required for user managers and staff members in units outside a direct reporting relationship to the TPP initiative leader and project owners. Recognizing that many user organizational variations exist, beginning-to-end accountability for the strategic direction TPP initiative goals and objectives, operating concept, project concepts, and project execution is an absolute necessity.

System architects and project managers must report to the TPP initiative leader and project owners on a project basis to make beginning-to-end accountability a reality. This reporting relationship gives the TPP initiative leader and project owners the right to make final decisions on everything relating to the project—scope, concept, requirements, schedule, and other considerations—except for the technical infrastructure and development guidelines that are under control of the chief information officer. Therefore, the TPP initiative leader and the project owners can and should be evaluated on the performance of system architects and

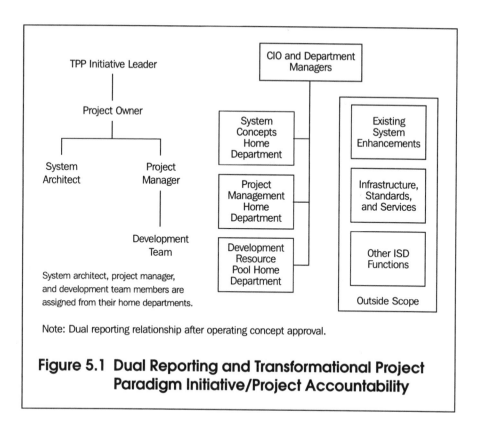

Figure 5.1 Dual Reporting and Transformational Project Paradigm Initiative/Project Accountability

project managers who report to them from concept formulation through project execution (see Figure 5.1.).

System architects, project managers, and development team members always report administratively to their respective system concepts, project management, and development resource pool home department managers. This arrangement allows their administrative managers flexibility to assign personnel appropriately to meet job demands. The arrangement benefits the TPP initiative leader and project owners by not leaving them with the awkward job of trying to place people who have completed their work and have no place to go. The benefits for ISD team members, as well as for management and the company, become obvious.

System architects and project managers, receiving direction from two sources, find that the communications usually contain different content.

The TPP initiative leader and project owners will discuss business-related topics, in contrast to direction given by the chief information officer and information systems division (ISD) home department managers that will consist of technically oriented matters.

Making Dual Reporting Work

The Transformational Project Paradigm (TPP) assumes that matrix management will be used where applicable which, by its nature, requires *dual reporting*. The TPP initiative leader reports to or is a member of senior management under the formal organization. The project owners, who are likely to be senior functional managers, report to the TPP initiative leader for all transformational project work, while reporting to a senior manager within the formal organizational structure for their other responsibilities. User functional managers and specialized staff members report to the project owners for transformational project work, while continuing to report to their managers within the formal organizational structure for their other responsibilities. Information systems division (ISD) system architects and project managers report to the TPP initiative leader or to project owners during transformational project work, while continuing to report administratively to their home department managers under the formal ISD organizational structure. Development team staff members report to the project manager, while reporting administratively to their ISD manager. The additional matrix reporting dimension does not require changes in the user formal organizational structure to be successful.

Under this initiative/project matrix form, the TPP initiative leader and project owners oversee the transformational project work and are responsible for its success or failure. Their authority to call the shots must exist for them to be held accountable and to prevent operating and project concepts from being pulled apart by politics. The status quo, not business transformation, prevails when separate interests govern.

Information systems division (ISD) system architects, project managers, and development team members can be assigned full time to transformational project work because projects make up their entire work responsibilities. Transformational Project Paradigm (TPP) initiative leaders, project owners, user functional managers, and specialized staff members have responsibilities within their organizational reporting structures in addition to the TPP initiative. Continuing operations must proceed to meet normal requirements while the TPP initiative leader, project owners, functional managers, and staff members devote their energies to TPP work.

The split between transformational project work and other responsibilities creates conflicting goals for senior management in assignment of user personnel. Senior management must set policies that support the need for handling normal operations of the company, while providing job continuity and stability for user managers and staff assigned to transformational project work. A promising future encourages good performers to devote their maximum energies to a TPP initiative and to their continuing responsibilities.

The Project Owner, Project Manager, and Line Authority

The project owner and project manager perform related but different lateral project coordination roles after the system architect completes the project concept. The TPP initiative leader should grant *de facto line authority* to the project owner over user managers, in respect to transformational project work within the scope of the project concept, to preserve beginning-to-end accountability. The project owner should be responsible for *negotiating* issues with managers at other companies within the project scope, with assistance from the TPP initiative leader, as required. Thus, the project owner exercises authority from an established position or as a negotiator. In contrast, the project manager has direct authority over the development team but must exercise her integrating role with users through recognized expertise in appliying technical solutions to business problems.

Between them, the project owner and project manager must be able to resolve conflicts among the various units, making sure that the project concept remains intact. They must be able to differentiate conflicts that relate to a user department manager's valid concern about workability from those that arise from placing a unit's desires above maintaining the integrity of the project concept. A project concept must not be pulled apart by politics.

Don Rossmoore, a consultant who works with senior managers at high-technology organizations, describes the essential need for effective project leadership toward this end: "Talented leaders can tap the potential of teams to share information, ideas, and enthusiasm without letting them get bogged down in politics. They are the missing link in today's flatter, team-oriented organizations."[7]

Trust and Collaboration

Trust and collaboration are crucial to make dual reporting work. Participants must work openly with one another toward a common end to achieve the level of understanding necessary for creative contributions. No alternative exists to the trust and collaboration requirement because systems work consists of thought and the ability to recreate in another's mind a common understanding of issues, ideas, options, and constraints. Andrew Grove describes the necessity for trust in the dual reporting environment:

> Trust in no way relates to an organizational principle but instead to an aspect of the corporate culture, something about which much has been written in recent years. Put simply, it is a set of values and beliefs, as well as familiarity with the way things are done and should be done in a company. The point is that a strong and positive corporate culture is absolutely essential if dual reporting and decision-making by peers are to work.[8]

Dual reporting requires effective collaboration that can only be built upon trust. Stanley Davis and Paul Lawrence, authors of a classic book on matrix reporting, describe the integral nature of trust to collaboration:

> To achieve collaboration, the needed ingredient is trust. Individuals and groups must learn to rely on each other and to accept each other's judgments when these are based on unique competence and knowledge. Without trust, the organization quickly reverts back to a reliance on chain-of-command authority.[9]

Trust and collaboration clearly are crucial to dual reporting and thus to the success of cross-boundary transformational project work itself.

Infrastructure Issue Resolution

Control over the technical infrastructure and resolution of related issues is a vital part of a chief information officer's responsibility and accountability. Infrastructure control is one of the topics included in a survey of 5,000 information technology executives who are members of a Price Waterhouse international Computer Opinion Panel, and of a further related research program conducted in 102 major corporations throughout the world that have appointed information technology directors. The survey finds that although a large majority of companies has a centrally controlled infrastructure, severe problems arise in practice about its acceptance at approximately one-half of those companies:

> A large majority of companies already divide their information technology into user-controlled applications, and a centrally controlled infrastructure. ... In practice, however, users' resentments of infrastructure constraints, and users' go-it-alone practices, are causing severe problems for at least half of those providing corporate infrastructures. ... Forty-seven percent state decentralized user activity is causing serious infrastructure problems.[10]

The Transformational Project Paradigm (TPP) framework addresses the infrastructure contention issue by calling for negotiation between the chief information officer, and the TPP initiative leader and project owners. As noted above, the latter two principals must negotiate issues with managers outside their control, in this case the chief information officer. The objective is to avoid the extremes of infrastructure dictation by the chief information officer and fragmentation of it by a TPP initiative or related projects.

When Dual Reporting Fails

Companies that cannot make dual reporting work, with responsibility and accountability resting with the TPP initiative leader and project owners, pay a high price:

- Effective delegation is lost: The chief executive-led senior management team loses its ability to grant to an individual the authority to execute a strategic TPP initiative, thus giving up the ability to hold a single leader accountable for results.
- Systems are developed either by users or by information systems divisions (ISDs): When information systems are either defined and developed separately by users or by ISDs, the disadvantages of piecemeal systems in the first case and of unresponsiveness in the second become disruptive.
- More chief information officer and staff turnover takes place: If systems are developed by ISD, the total responsibility assumed unfairly by the chief information officer and ISD staff members causes more turnover in their ranks as large projects go awry. This reduces the ability of a company to implement mainstream systems necessary to improve its competitive strength.
- Default is to keep old systems: Although much planning may be done for new transformational systems development, the lack of accountability and capability causes companies to keep their old functionally oriented systems, since by default they can only continue with outmoded concepts.

Establishing a Positive Work Environment

The chief information officer, his department managers, the TPP initiative leader, and project owners must establish a non-threatening work environment that promotes creativity, trust, and sharing of technical advances and business techniques. The environment must be consistent with the nature of systems work where knowledge and ability to handle mentally challenging work is essential, recognizing that significant contributions emanate from the intellects of the people involved. Failure to establish a viable means for individuals to make creative contributions can result in loss of valuable employee input.

Alan Loy McGinnis, an authority on psychological motivation, calls our attention to a statement by Bill Hewlett, one of the two founders of Hewlett-Packard, about the importance of a constructive business environment: "Our policy flows from the belief that men and women want to do a good job, a creative job, and that if they are provided with the proper environment they will do so."[11]

Although some assume that only designers perform technical conceptual work, project managers and development team members exercise this ability in order to visualize and understand thoroughly the work at hand, an essential systems development ingredient. Incorporating creativity into the process for all participants requires management flexibility in the form of openness to new ideas and innovative ways to resolve troublesome problems, and objective consideration and evaluation of creative contributions. It further mandates acceptance of individuals who may not follow the group's line of thought, but may offer innovative or breakthrough ideas, and kindness in the workplace, remembering that people need to feel that they have a future if they offer their best efforts for evaluation.

Establishment of Information Systems Division Home Departments

Companies often manage an ISD like a functional department with respect to systems definition, design, and development—it isn't a functional department. Information systems divisions (Isds) contain skilled technical staff members whose purpose is to assist company management and users in reaching their business goals and objectives. The majority of ISD's project work, with the notable exception of infrastructure development and year 2000 compliance projects, is done directly for business users. The chief information officer, to ensure technical compatibility companywide, establishes the standards, development guidelines, and the infrastructure within which system architects, project managers, and development team members must operate. (Information systems division standards, development guidelines, and infrastructure are outside the scope of this book.)

Support of a creative, conceptual thought process for all aspects of transformational project work requires an in-house business setting that offers the opportunity for individual and group contributions to be evaluated by managers objectively, in a non-threatening manner. Frederick Brooks cites the importance of supporting creative individuals: "If one believes . . . that creativity comes from individuals and not from structures or processes, then a central question facing the software manager is how to design structure and process so as to enhance, rather than inhibit, creativity and initiative.[12]

Establishment of system concepts, project management, and development resource pool home departments (often called centers of excellence) for system architects, project managers, and development team members can aid the creative, conceptual thought process by providing the appropriate setting for their respective specialties. The chief information officer, the three ISD home department managers, the Transformational Project Paradigm (TPP) initiative leaders, and the project owners will need to work together to establish an overall environment conducive to creative work by key user and technical participants.

Although the topic of how to set up a non-threatening environment to encourage creativity extends beyond the scope of this book, McGinnis offers twelve rules that may serve as a helpful guideline:

1. Expect the best from people you lead.
2. Make a thorough study of the other person's needs.
3. Establish high standards for excellence.
4. Create an environment where failure is not fatal.
5. If they are going anywhere near where you want to go, climb on other people's bandwagons.
6. Employ models to encourage success.
7. Recognize and applaud achievement.
8. Employ a mixture of positive and negative reinforcement.
9. Appeal sparingly to the competitive urge.
10. Place a premium on collaboration.
11. Build into the group an allowance for storms.
12. Take steps to keep your own motivation high.[13]

Fosters Capability to Perform Broad and Complex Work

Limited research has been consistent in showing that perceived expertise and trustworthiness are the two most important factors in establishing professional credibility in an organizational setting, according to academic researchers Barbara Bashein and Lynne Markus in a *Sloan Management Review* article on information technology specialist credibility.[14] The importance of expert power is indicated from a survey of 146 project managers and individual contributors who worked on projects in a matrix environment, as reported in the *Project Management Journal:*

The category which ranked highest of the seven power based was expert power. Outstanding project managers are powerful because they have a reputation for being knowledgeable both about the project and about ways to get it done. There was little disagreement about this ranking from respondents.[15]

Transformational project formulation and execution require a much greater level of knowledge and skill than do projects where only one functional or process area is involved. Expertise becomes a crucial influence factor in leading a project.

Bashein and Markus observe in their *Sloan Management Review* article that establishing trustworthiness is often neglected. They report that research has identified four dimensions of perceived trustworthiness: similarity and likeability, prolonged interaction, appropriate behavior, and consistent behavior.[16] The TPP framework promotes system architect and project manager user-perceived trustworthiness by having them report to the TPP initiative leader or project owners; credibility from the business standpoint becomes integral to personal performance.

System architects and project managers must become familiar with business application areas and knowledgeable about related technical solutions to be effective in cross-boundary communication. In addition to required knowledge, they often need training and experience in communication methods to reach the required level of overall expertise.

Even though packages and easier programming techniques are becoming ever more available, the need for well-trained technical people to: (1) conceive operating and project concepts across business areas, (2) to understand how those concepts tie in with the strategic direction, and (3) to comprehend and work with a myriad of technical choices goes far beyond assistance gained from packages, reusable code, and other programming advances. Rockart and Short comment on this new level of complexity and greater challenge:

> First, with regard to systems development, even those systems in which the line is heavily involved require greater competence and skills on the part of the information technology organization. The technical design, programming, and operation of business-critical, complex systems present a far greater challenge than do systems of previous eras. Today's integrated, cross-functional product delivery systems require database,

project management, telecommunications, and other skills not previously demanded of information technology personnel.[17]

Information systems division (ISD) home departments provide an essential structure to support all aspects of expertise development. Specialized departments are known for their strength in developing such expertise. They allow personnel to progress in their own specialty, enabling people to perform increasingly complex assignments. System architects, project managers, and development team members have an opportunity to learn from their colleagues in actual work situations, and to continue with the same kind of work. Development of creative and technically trained system architects and project managers capable of performing transformational project work is vital for effective deployment of advanced information technology.

Since studies have shown that the level of talent applied to software development is the strongest predictor of its outcomes,[18] it makes good business sense to create separate departments within ISD for system architects, project managers, and development team members.

Provides Career Growth and Stability

Home departments give project personnel stability and the opportunity for career growth without leaving their specialties. System architects and project managers are offered both *security*—there will be a place to return after finishing the work—and *growth*—opportunities to be assigned project work at levels of increasing complexity. Working one's way up on progressively complex assignments within a skill area is highly effective in developing one's understanding and proficiency.

Offers Motivation to Complete Projects and Promotes Assignment Flexibility

The worry about where one will go after completing the current assignment *is a major demotivator to completion of an assignment.* Availability to be assigned to a wide variety of projects is better for project personnel than assignment to an ISD department organized by user function. A particular user area can lose its priority for project work and may not be granted additional projects at the time staff is available.

The structure makes it easy to assemble project teams to address cross-boundary needs. When a team member completes an assignment, that person simply returns to the home department for training or another assignment. Specific user functional needs can be handled without development staff being permanently assigned to those areas with an ISD management structure to match.

Fosters Cross-Boundary Knowledge

Transformational projects cut across boundaries. Creating separate home departments in ISDs for system architects and project managers, regardless of user function, promotes varied business knowledge by giving them an opportunity to work across different business areas. Moreover, they can attend training classes together and associate with one another. Certain architects and project managers can specialize in one- or two-user functional areas such as production, distribution, finance, or marketing to provide in-depth knowledge as needed.

Supports Uniform Development Guidelines and Infrastructure Control

Since all project team members are based in ISDs and report ultimately to the chief information officer for technical guidance, infrastructure control, and standards, the same criteria can be used on every assignment, thus fostering system development consistency across the company. Consider this observation from chief information officers who employ centers of excellence:

> Imagine: IS staff, skilled in a particular product or methodology, apply their brand of expertise every time they move to another project.

Eventually, that one technology or architecture becomes the norm throughout the organization. No arm-pulling, no politics.[19]

System architects and project managers will support the need for a common infrastructure and follow the procedure for requesting additions or revisions to it on every assignment because of their reporting relationships to the chief information officer. This means of organization and responsibility reduces the likelihood of fragmentation.

Organizational Focus on Transformational Project Work

The Transformational Project Paradigm (TPP) home department structure is geared to crucial transformational project work, as depicted in Figure 5.2. It also provides for other assignments. Successful managers focus on critical success factors while keeping other operations efficient. The chart shows how TPP home departments support that goal.

System Architects and Project Managers

Development of expert system architects and project managers is the *largest single factor in increasing the capacity of a company to formulate and develop transformational projects.* In fact, a company should not embark upon transformational project work until the chief information officer is satisfied that he has system architects and project managers capable of handling the assignments. A company can spend huge sums on information technology and never realize return from successful transformational system projects unless this personnel need is met.

The system architect assembles ideas, relevant internal and outside data, requirements, and constraints into a workable, conceptual design in sufficient detail to provide the basis for technical specifications. This conceptual design forms the mental creation and documentation bridge

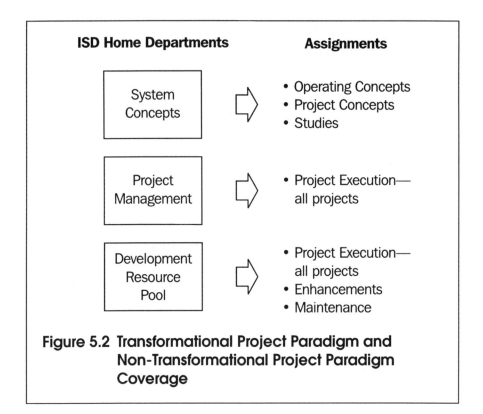

Figure 5.2 Transformational Project Paradigm and Non-Transformational Project Paradigm Coverage

between business objectives and the ability of a project manager and development team to realize those objectives through project execution. Without this documentation bridge, a company can remain locked in a recurring cycle of business planning for needed systems without ever being able to bring those plans into reality through working systems.

A project manager coordinates system development with all interested parties, addresses relevant issues and problems, and leads development team members in project execution within the guidelines of cost, schedule, and quality performance objectives. A system architect can generate an appropriate conceptual and documented design, but a company cannot carry it forward to realization without the expertise of a thoroughly trained and competent project manager.

Rather than system architects and project managers being an extra operating expense, their use can obviate the need for intermediate-level management positions in information systems divisions (ISDs). Otherwise, ISD functional managers must supervise the technical personnel. This responsibility is transferred to the project managers under the TPP structure.

Bridging the User/Information Systems Division Communication Gap

System architects and project managers *must* be able to communicate about technological issues on a business level with *all* contributors in order to tie business practices to technological solutions. The architects, in particular, must be capable of grasping high-level objectives and of seeing their implications with respect to technical capabilities. They need a combination of applied creativity and sound conceptual thinking to generate ideas leading to the best alternatives, along with an objective analytical ability to determine the value and workability of each.

The architects must be able to describe alternative technical solutions to the business managers to achieve two results: to ascertain the pros and cons of each alternative from the standpoint of the business objectives and to open new possibilities to enhance the business objectives based on technical capabilities.

This joining of objectives with the technical solution becomes the key attribute to a successful system concept that can maximize the impact of advanced information technology, given effective project execution.

Organizing the Departments

The first step is to recruit managers for each of the system concepts and project management departments from internal or external sources. The *system concepts manager* must have performed conceptual design work for large, implemented systems. The *project management manager* must have led development teams to successful conclusion of such system projects. Both must be technically up to date and have the communication ability necessary to assist as needed in issue resolution between users and ISDs. The two managers act as consultants to their staff members for complex matters that arise during assignments. This counsel gives system architects and project managers additional support in their knowledge and skill areas, realizing that ISD department managers do not carry accountability for success or failure of their staff transformational project endeavors.

The second step is to fill the system architect and project manager positions, either from internal or external sources. Primary considerations are the ability to create workable solutions from a diverse set of facts and circumstances for system architects and the ability to manage a group of technical specialists toward successful project conclusion for project managers.

System architects and project managers must acquire, for Transformational Project Paradigm (TPP) project work, extensive background and abilities. They need in-depth knowledge of TPP initiative goals and objectives as they relate to advanced information technology. They must understand company business practices in the application areas and comparable practices in other companies. They can communicate effectively with company business managers and specialized technical personnel. They possess proven ability to operate effectively on prior complex projects.

All system architects and project managers must have these essential attributes to be effective, regardless of whether they are employees, work on a consulting basis within the ISD home department structure, or work on a fully outsourced basis from an equivalent of the system concepts and project management home departments.

Separate System Concepts and Project Management Home Departments

Separate system concepts and project management home departments are better than a combined department for three reasons: to address different system architect and project manager talents, to facilitate initial studies and proposals, and to promote focus and accountability for applying one's energies to the task at hand.

A system architect's strength lies in creating a design, whereas a project manager's strength lies in executing the design through effective management of people to produce a working system. Frederick Brooks notes the difference in roles and delineates the importance of a clean boundary between a system architect's and project manager's work:

> This role [system architect] is a full-time job, and only on the smallest teams can it be combined with that of the team manager. The architect is like the director and the manager like the producer of a motion picture. ... To make the architect's crucial task even conceivable, it is necessary to separate the architecture, the definition of the product as perceivable by the user, from its implementation. Architecture versus implementation defines a clean boundary between parts of the design task, and there is plenty of work on each side of it.[20]

The second reason to have separate system concepts and project management departments is to facilitate initial studies and proposals prepared by system architects from ongoing project execution work led by project managers on previously authorized projects. System architects need to be available for studies and proposal work that might not result in an approved project. By having them in a separate department, it is easier to assign them to initial study work than it would be if they were combined with the project managers in a single unit.

Separate system concepts and project management home departments have a third subtle advantage. Separation promotes focus and accountability to apply one's energies to the task at hand. Locating the two types of specialties in separate departments minimizes departure from the assigned task, a problem in creative work. Edward de Bono stresses the need for a creative person to stay with the task at hand:

> Focus discipline is extremely important. Creative people often earn themselves a bad name by refusing to focus on the task that has been set before them. They want to have brilliant ideas about some other focus. ... Focus discipline is probably the most important of all disciplines.[21]

The system concepts and project management home departments formalize system architect and project manager positions in the information systems division (ISD) organizational structure. This encourages staff members to direct their work toward fulfillment of TPP initiative and project goals and objectives.

Development Resource Pool

The resource pool can be considered a center of excellence for smaller companies, or be subdivided into development team specialties. Sources for setting up centers of excellence within the resource pool are widely available, as indicated by the 70 percent of Fortune 1000 companies that have implemented them in some form. The centers are organized by specific skill areas—systems analyst, programmer, and technical specialist—to foster the variety of abilities necessary to perform development work and to set up groups of a manageable size.

Similar Organizational Modes

The ISD home department organization under the TPP is similar to the resource pool organization at IBM's Integrated Systems Solutions Corporation Center at Bethesda, Maryland (United States). That organization has contract/project managers who draw technical personnel from a resource pool for the full execution time of the project. During that time, programmers and other technical specialists report only to the project manager in respect to project activities. The TPP organization differs from the Integrated Systems Solutions Corporation Center in two respects. Project managers reside in one department with specialty areas of concentration within that department, whereas the Integrated Systems Solutions Corporation Center project managers work in separate departments for outsourcing, fulfillment, and public sector contracts; and system architects reside in a separate department, whereas the Integrated Systems Solutions Corporation Center does not identify this capability.[22]

The TPP organization is also similar to a center of excellence model, which, *Computerworld* reports, 70 percent of all Fortune 1000 companies have implemented in some form.[23] Texas Instruments, an early adopter of the center of excellence model, has set up seventeen centers, including infrastructure specialties, in its overall information services division.[24] A system concept center is not identified within the seventeen. Establishing centers of excellence can be a significant change in many information systems organizations, but it offers important advantages. Tom Shipley, vice president of Gartner Group, Inc.'s Management of Information Technology Group in Austin, Texas (United States), asserts: "Centers can sometimes be the only way to manage a flat organization. They also let you deliver skills and resources to a project just in time, leverage economies of scale and propagate an architecture throughout the enterprise."[25]

Changing the ISD to a home department, or center of excellence model, is not an easy task. Texas Instrument's officials found that "the heart of the problem really lay with the fact that we were changing the whole belief that the boss should be the one who determines how much people get paid, and what and where they get trained," according to Steve Lyle, the firm's director of Business Excellence for Information Technology. "We found the biggest cause of disaster is when you don't dispel [IS] middle management fears."[26]

The TPP organizational structure clarifies and separates the important role of system architects, which differs from the Integrated Systems Solutions Corporation Center and center of excellence models, as noted above. Although a project owner can be designated as the person accountable for project success or failure in either of the other models, the TPP model makes it mandatory to achieve beginning-to-end accountability.

Outsourcing

A company that chooses to outsource the equivalent of the ISD system concepts, project management, and development resource pool home departments will need to treat the outsourced system architects and project managers as if they were internal staff members under the Transformational Project Paradigm (TPP). This holds even if the outsourced consultants and contractors are based at a remote location. Responsibility and accountability for TPP initiative project success or failure *rests with the TPP initiative leader and project owners* regardless of the project team sourcing arrangement.

System architects and project managers must be given complete access to TPP initiative and project goals and objectives under any sourcing arrangement, and they must be considered as professional members of a company's staff in order for them to perform their roles. Although a factor in prompting outsourcing can be stated as, "People want to buy knowledge, not develop it themselves,"[27] understanding, not knowledge, is the crucial need in designing and executing transformational projects. This understanding can only be gained through intimate study of and access to goals, objectives, and business practices of a specific company. Thus, a company that uses outsourcing for transformational projects must be prepared to divulge related, critical matters needed for transformational project work to members of the outsourcing firm.

When a company chooses partial outsourcing because it does not have all of the expertise necessary to proceed with transformational projects, the chief information officer can evaluate and select expert personnel from outside consultant and contractor sources, and integrate them into the TPP structure. Outsourced system architects, project managers, and development team members will be assigned to the system concepts, project management, and development resource pool departments, respectively. The chief information officer and the department managers should utilize the talents of consulting and contract personnel as if they were in-house staff members; TPP initiative leaders and project owners should treat them in exactly the same way.

The *Sloan Management Review* suggests selective outsourcing for technically immature activities when additional expertise is required where, the article asserts, total outsourcing engenders significant risk. Technical maturity, according to the authors' definition, is a measure of the degree to which a company can specify its requirements to a vendor.[28] Transformational projects, by their nature, have a low degree of technical maturity because formulating operating and project concepts and determining requirements are part of the overall process.

6

The Management Reporting System

In many cases, the project organization is superimposed on an ongoing organization, and its management control system is superimposed on the management control system of that organization. ... a special management control system must be developed for the project, and it must mesh at certain points with the system of the ongoing organization.

Robert N. Anthony, *The Management Control Function*

The chief information officer, as the executive most familiar with the nature of systems work, should be responsible for specifying and developing the Transformational Project Paradigm (TPP) management reporting system with support from the chief executive-led senior management team. The chief information officer serves as project owner of the TPP management reporting system project, with chief financial officer counsel on financial matters and control. Support of the chief information officer from the chief executive-led management team is crucial because incorporating this type of reporting into the formal management control system can be a major change for any company. Robert Anthony, a renowned expert in management reporting, observes that the driving force for a new management control system must come from senior management because it is unlikely that operating managers will voluntarily embrace, let alone be enthusiastic advocates, of the control system.[1]

The chief executive-led senior management team will need to evaluate the extent of transformational project work going forward, the size of the expenditures in relation to other costs, and the risk of insufficient management attention to determine the sophistication level of the TPP management reporting system. The level can range from being an official, specialized part of the total management reporting system to being a one-time-use system. The size of the development effort and tie-in points with the existing system depend, in large part, on the level of sophistication required.

Basis for Transformational Project Paradigm Management Reporting

An inherent conflict exists between having a single budget number in advance of work performance and systems work estimates being refined as a result of doing the work itself, as discussed in Chapter 2. Cost measurement against advance budget numbers can show cost overruns when they do not in fact exist and cause project participants to be evaluated unfairly. On the other hand, the budgeting in retrospect that flows logically from the nature of systems work provides no means for control or evaluation. Unfortunately, the nature of systems work prevents even a most likely estimate within the cost range.

What can be done? The budgetary commitment can become a range that narrows, barring obstacles or external changes, as milestones are reached. Thus, budgets should reflect a high and low plan. Even so, the reporting system will need to provide for approved exceptions that cannot be foreseen when the range is estimated. The next work stage and the remaining subproject or project will need to be reestimated at the end of each stage.

Management reporting cannot replace milestone planning and review meetings. Hans Thamhain, a well-known researcher on technology-based project management and team building, has found from a study of over 180 multinational projects, mostly product/service developments with budgets averaging $1.2 million, that the *stage-gate process* has gained wide acceptance for managing complex projects, especially those requiring multifunctional integrations. He also has found that one of the prime objectives for using stage-gate processes is to make the project cycle and its performance more predictable, that is, to minimize downstream uncertainty, risk, and complications. Each stage leads to a *gate* that defines the specific criteria and results that must be met before the project can proceed to the next stage.[2]

Project versus Functional Budgeting

Marie Scotto, project management consultant and author, contends that "using functional budgeting concepts on project budgets renders the most sophisticated project management approach ineffective."[3] Transformational Project Paradigm (TPP) management reporting requires a *budgeting basis* that is *separate and different* from the annual budgeting cycle for functional units. Annual budgeting is an excellent vehicle for management reporting of repetitive, short-duration work that has comparable prior history, such as shipping products or collecting invoices, but it does not apply to transformational project work. Budgeting must be *consistent with the way the way work is done*, or it cannot be used to measure the results.

Functional departments usually have comparable current and prior-year budgets to refer to as a starting point for preparing next year's budget. In contrast, system architects and project managers rarely have comparable project records to use as a starting point for budgeting a new project. Two reasons exist for this problem—every project is unique in whole or in part, and few companies maintain project records. Complicating the situation further is the lack of specifications at the beginning of the effort and undiscovered rework during development and testing. At best, estimates can only be educated guesses at early stages followed by informed, reestimated ranges for budgeting purposes as the project progresses.

In contrast to functional budgets, TPP initiative and project budgets *encompass unique, multiyear work efforts.* Instead of annual, functional objectives against which to measure progress for money spent, projects have objectives that are realized at two points—at the end of each implemented subproject and at total project implementation time. Neither point relates to an annual budgeting cycle in respect to timing. As a result of this timing discrepancy and of the need to reestimate budgets periodically throughout the life of the project, transformational project budgeting *must be separated from functional budgeting* in the way managers think about measuring actual progress against plan.

The nature of transformational project work *creates a loss of budgetary control* if the costs are considered as operating expense within an annual budget cycle. Annual budget numbers for a large project soon become out of date, which, in effect, means that the *project is running out of control* in respect to management reporting. To maintain budgetary control for such work, the project manager should reestimate ranges for near-term work periodically as milestones are achieved and more specifics become known about future work. The chief information officer is responsible for setting project milestone review frequency and for determining reestimating points as part of the development guidelines.

The initial annual budget for functional units is a real budget for comparison purposes, whereas only the most recent official reestimate can provide real budget numbers for transformational project work. Although use of the most recent budget as the basis for performance evaluation might deviate from company practices, the alternative would be to evaluate information systems division (ISD) project team personnel unfairly because of the inherent nature of systems work. A budget must represent realizable targets in order to be an effective control mechanism.

Reporting Levels and Budgeting

The Transformational Project Paradigm (TPP) initiative budget range should originate at the time the operating concept is approved; the TPP initiative leader becomes responsible for the budget at that time. Related project budget ranges should originate at project concept approval time and be assigned to the project owner by the TPP initiative leader. Thus, *two levels* of management reporting—the initiative level and the project level—should be maintained for a TPP initiative, with project detail tying back to the overall initiative authorization. A revision history should be retained at both levels as changes are approved and disapproved throughout the life of the initiative.

Transformational Project Paradigm initiative and ensuing project costs should be capitalized starting at operating concept approval time, the point at which technological feasibility is established and management becomes committed to the endeavor. Transformational Project Paradigm (TPP) initiative costs, from the point of operating concept approval through cutover of all related systems, should be capitalized for management reporting purposes regardless of whether such costs are classified as capital or expense for financial and tax reporting purposes. The ISD budget should contain an operating expense category for research, conceptual design, and proposal preparation work related to formulating operating concepts.

Reporting System Requirements

The TPP management reporting system makes accountability real because it *aligns and clarifies the flow of responsibility* from the chief executive-led senior management team through to the TPP initiative leader and project owners. Transformational Project Paradigm (TPP) managers, to be held accountable, must receive in a timely manner the following three types of reports that are similar to those needed by other managers: visibility of actual progress to plan to monitor progress, status of resources to make realistic commitments, and information to identify problems to take or recommend corrective action. The data collection and reporting flow is shown in Figure 6.1.

Although the reports for TPP managers are similar to those needed by other managers, the basis for designing the TPP management reporting system must be consistent with the characteristics of transformational project systems work. The extent of and method for data collection must take as little time as possible away from project team work efforts while gathering sufficient data to produce the reports required for management review.

Actual Progress to Plan

Meaningful reporting of progress against plan is essential. Suppose a six-month subproject portion of a two-year project has a high-range budget of $500,000. At the end of the first three months the actual cost is $250,000. Does this mean that the subproject is on track from the high-range budget standpoint? It is impossible to tell from those two numbers. The team might be 10, 50, 80, or any other percent complete with the subproject work. One of two solutions must be employed to learn the actual status: either define planned milestone results by time period and report achievement of them along with actual cost comparisons to high- and low-range budget amounts, or use the earned value method in conjunction with the budget ranges. This method does not replace the need for milestone reviews.

Quentin Fleming and Joel Koppelman, experts in project reporting, describe the objectives of the earned value method:

> Earned value is a "strategic" trend indicator. It seeks answers to a number of questions. If we stay on this present performance course, where will we

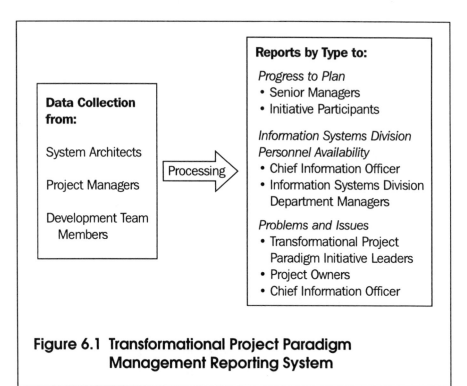

Figure 6.1 Transformational Project Paradigm Management Reporting System

end up? How much money will we need to complete the project? How long will it take to get there? This is the purpose of earned value measurement. It looks for a monthly performance position, and the long-term direction of the project. ...

Earned value projects have two primary areas of focus. The first is on the performance to the planned schedule. ... The second area of focus is on cost performance.[4]

Fleming and Koppelman add that planned cost expenditures against actual costs formats should be restricted to management of funding, not project performance.[5]

The TPP initiative leader and project owners are accountable for reviewing the reestimates, as furnished by the system architects and project managers with counsel, as needed, from the chief information officer and the ISD department managers. Once approved, the reestimates must become the basis for evaluating progress against plan because only the most recent estimate is suitable for control purposes, using either the milestone or earned value method. Original and prior estimates should be kept on record, of course, to provide a complete budget and time history of the initiative and related projects.

Realistic Commitments

Russell Archibald visualizes a desired state where project-driven organizations will take timely action to provide resources when needed, based on forecasts of people, money, and other resource requirements from information provided by summarizing the plans of all projects under way.[6] The chief information officer and ISD department managers must know the current status of ISD personnel commitments by assignment, skill, and time period in order to fulfill their responsibilities to provide qualified technical personnel for transformational projects. Transformational Project Paradigm (TPP) initiative leaders and project owners must know the availability of ISD personnel before making their initial commitments concerning work to be accomplished. Forecast reporting that *summarizes current and planned assignments* is required to avoid making unrealistic commitments. Costly symptoms of overcommitment are common in information systems organizations: transfer of key personnel from one incomplete project to another, stopping and restarting projects, and overworked staff members.

Incorporating the ability to make realistic commitments into the TPP management reporting system serves two purposes: to avoid taking on new work where the resources are not or cannot be made available within the required time period, and to provide an informed means for effective assignment of required resources to ongoing projects.

The TPP management reporting system must include an efficient way to collect data from ISD staff members, one that reflects the combination of time spent on current projects for progress reporting purposes, and for planned time, from them or from their managers, to show future availability.

Problem Identification and Corrective Action

At every stage of transformational project work, problems can crop up seemingly out of the blue as the reality of detailed and complex work encounters a fluid and dynamic business environment. Even the most specific requirements can become ambiguous and incomplete when actual development work is under way. A manager's ability to identify problems and take appropriate corrective action is made even more difficult by the lack of physical evidence of progress that is inherent in the nature of systems work. Three things need to be done to foster problem identification under the umbrella of accountability for project results:

1. Promote understanding of what is taking place among all participants, especially among the Transformational Project Paradigm (TPP) initiative leader, project owners, system architects, and project managers. The TPP management reporting system and related progress meetings will promote understanding at an official level. A good working relationship among these principals fosters informal communication to enhance the level of understanding.

2. Evaluate objectively all feasible alternatives. This holds true from the point of the original operating concept through cutover of the final related system. Objective evaluation requires understanding of the issues at hand plus an orientation toward solving problems in an optimal way.

3. Establish an environment of trust. "We are all in this together" is factually true in a systems development environment. Unlike working in a situation where physical items can be handed to the next person, documentation and technical components given by one person to another are of little value unless mutual understanding of the thinking behind them exists.

Having established the reporting system, progress meetings, and a productive, supportive environment, the most important problems must receive priority attention. Neal Whitten, consultant and author in the project management and employee development areas, observes that high-priority problems might change throughout the life of a project, but the level of attention they receive will have a major impact on the health of a project. He adds that if the most important problems are not solved first, the project and its participants will *drift*, having serious negative effects on productivity, schedules, morale, quality, and the level of rework. Drift may even cause eventual death of a project.[7] Whitten recommends how to address project problems:

Step 1. Pinpoint Priorities: Identify and prioritize the most important problems.

Step 2. Assign One Owner: Assign an owner to each priority problem.

Step 3. Commit to a Course of Action: Develop a plan that will successfully resolve each priority problem.

Step 4. Review Progress Daily: Review the priority problems daily.[8]

The TPP supports problem identification and resolution through beginning-to-end accountability and a productive working environment. The focus of the TPP, however, is on *problem prevention* fostered by alignment of four key management practices—beginning-to-end accountability, cross-boundary coordination, ISD home departments, and the management reporting system—with the nature of systems work.

Part III

Transformational Project Work

7

Creating the Operating and Project Concepts

Technology is becoming a commodity: what matters are the application concepts. Concepts are every bit as important as finance, raw materials, labor and energy. It is not enough to rely on "me-too" copying or the haphazard use of creative intelligence. We need to take concepts very seriously indeed.

Edward de Bono, *Sur/petition*

Competition has become a battle of *concepts* in the Information Age. A company's ability to formulate superior concepts and to implement them successfully in a timely manner through transformational projects is tantamount to achieving the promise of information technology.

To recap, a concept is much broader in scope than an idea. An *idea* is merely a single thought without regard for workability and interrelationships. A *concept*, in contrast, is only viable when all related business and technical aspects mesh into a workable solution on a broad and detailed basis. Concept formulation requires knowledge of the business areas and technical possibilities, solutions achieved by other companies, and approaches taken in different, but concept-related application areas.

Concept formulation must take place before user requirements testing. Otherwise companies stay locked into applying technology to traditional ways of doing business. Advanced information technology capabilities expressed through superior concepts must be the driving force for transformational projects.

Let's look at how a company should approach development of superior concepts within a setting of accountability. For purposes of illustration, the approach assumes a single company without separate business units; the same principles would apply for companies using business units or other forms of organization. The following discussion establishes a process for adaptation by management to meet the unique demands of a company's situation.

Setting of Policies, Responsibilities, and Justification Guidelines

The chief executive has ultimate responsibility for the *strategic direction,* or *game plan,* an integral part of which is the *what* and *why* of all initiatives. The chief operating officer has ultimate responsibility for the *how, when,* and *where* of initiatives, which affect *company operations and services.* She can assume leadership of Transformational Project Paradigm (TPP) initiatives or delegate the leadership role to another senior manager. The chief information officer advises the chief executive-led senior management team about how advanced information technology capabilities might change initiative goals and objectives or create an opportunity for a new initiative.

The chief information officer has the final authority to assign system architects and project managers to TPP initiatives and projects, subject to negotiation with the TPP initiative leader and project owners. The chief information officer and his unit managers are best able to evaluate the conceptual and technical abilities of the two information systems division leads to accomplish the assignments effectively. The chief information officer is responsible for the standards, infrastructure, and development guidelines essential for consistency and long-term success of TPP initiatives.

A TPP initiative can be successful only *if the strategic direction is appropriate for the business environment and marketplace.* An initiative that produces directed but wrong results will do nothing positive for a company. Transformational Project Paradigm (TPP) initiative leaders, project owners, and team members must not be blamed for improper results that originate from poor strategic planning.

The Transformational Project Paradigm Initiative

We will assume that the TPP initiatives have now been identified and prioritized and that the chief executive-led senior management team has set goals and objectives. Each selected TPP initiative will have the following characteristics (as listed in Chapter 1):

- connects with strategic direction goals and objectives
- employs advanced information technology, including networking, to activate it
- operates across function, process, business unit, geographic, and/or company boundaries
- offers dramatic improvement in the way work can be performed through a superior concept to achieve growth, increased productivity, cost control, better utilization of assets, and/or higher customer satisfaction
- produces competitive value for an individual company or for an alliance of companies
- applies to business-critical application areas such as production and inventory control, order management, and financial reporting.

The Transformational Project Paradigm Initiative Leader and Project Owners

The TPP initiative leader assumes responsibility and accountability for *all* aspects of the TPP initiative after the chief executive-led senior management team defines its goals and objectives. Responsibilities include operating and project concept formulation, project execution, user personnel considerations, and current and fixed asset effects. The TPP initiative leader has the authority to delegate accountability for parts of the initiative represented by project business objectives to business managers who perform as project owners under her direction in respect to the initiative.

The TPP initiative leader, in participation with appointed project owners, sets forth the initiative's objectives in the level of detail necessary to serve as actionable project business objectives, the *what* of a TPP initiative at project level. The project concepts portray *how* related business objectives will be accomplished, following the same relationship to those objectives as the operating concept has to the goals and objectives of the TPP initiative.

Guided by actionable business objectives, the project owners are *accountable to the TPP initiative leader* for all aspects of their projects. In carrying out their responsibilities, project owners will need to include these factors for consideration: effects of advanced information technology deployment on business managers and staff members; impact on current and fixed assets, if applicable; present state of existing systems; ability of user and information systems division personnel to accomplish the required work; and interaction of the project with other business areas of the company. Since assignment of accountability is a significant step, care must be taken to ensure that new project owners are given the opportunity to assimilate all available and relevant background information.

Transformational Project Paradigm Initiative/ Project Justification Guidelines

Computerworld reports that methods to forecast benefits from growth opportunities and customer satisfaction are still in their infancy. Many companies are looking for new ways to gauge the costs and value of information systems including consideration of the business value-added method that measures information technology contribution not in dollars but by its support of key goals and metrics of functional groups. The main thing is to fuse information technology efforts to important targets and then look at how well those targets are met. The key is picking the best business goal. The method works best when an initiative has strong high-level support, routine operations are under control, and the business wants to grow. It should not be used in a heavily quantitative culture. The business value-added method should assist in aligning business goals and information technology by judging the latter with the yardstick of the former.[1]

Transformational project work requires additional justification guidelines either to supplement or replace widely used return on investment analyses. The chief financial officer should formulate the additional measurements that are appropriate for the goals and objectives of Transformational Project Paradigm (TPP) initiatives, with counsel from the chief information officer. It is likely that the guidelines will need to be refined as experience is gained and increased knowledge about new justification methods becomes available.

Assumptions Underlying the Operating and Project Concepts

In order for a TPP initiative to be successful, a company must be able to assign required personnel resources to it on a priority basis over a long period of time, while continuing to operate with existing systems enhanced to address short-term needs. A potential necessity to stabilize existing systems, perform extensive system revisions, initiate other large system efforts, or embark upon non-TPP initiatives that require the same resources must be evaluated with respect to diversion from the TPP endeavor.

The chief information officer and TPP initiative leader should evaluate at the outset the state of existing systems stability and the readiness of the user organization to support change. Conflicting or higher priority non-TPP initiatives must be identified and discussed openly in light of their potential impact on the TPP initiative. In addition, the chief information officer needs to evaluate technical resource availability and qualifications in cooperation with her home department managers. *The TPP initiative should either be given required priority and adequate personnel resources or should not be started until the required level of priority is granted and the necessary personnel resources are available.*

Consideration of User Personnel

Success of any initiative is more likely if user personnel, who contribute to or are affected by system implementation, support the endeavor. The TPP initiative leader and project owners must evaluate the effect that project implementation will have on user personnel, and consider the probable feelings of staff members. Understandably, no one wants to contribute to a project that will cause elimination of his job or a reduction of personal authority.

If the TPP initiative leader and project owners find that few want the endeavor to proceed, the likelihood of success will be low. Under this circumstance, they must take one or more of the following actions: (1) persuade the affected personnel of the endeavor's value and plan for their new roles during the transition, (2) revise the operating and project concepts in cooperation with the system architects based on feedback from the users, or (3) decide if staff changes will be required and advise those affected about the need for retraining and reassignment. *Advanced information technology deployment should not be the reason to lose good people, when retraining and reassignment can allow them the opportunity to continue to make effective and valuable contributions to the company.*

Use of Creative, Conceptual Thinking and Constructive Analysis

The creative process becomes the setting within which the operating and project concepts are defined. Successful project execution also requires this mode of thinking to resolve issues and problems that arise. The creative process flows from strategic TPP initiative goals and objectives through the operating concept, through project concepts, and through project execution, ending only with system cutover. Transformational Project Paradigm (TPP) initiative principals must be able to identify opportunities, weigh alternative courses of action, and address problems and issues by a combination of creative, conceptual thought and constructive analysis to ensure that related requirements are met. To do otherwise will contribute to disjointed or failed projects that do not realize the goals and objectives of the strategic direction TPP initiative.

Operating and project concept formulation requires a supportive environment that nurtures conceptual creativity in a context of accountability. Participants at all levels—from the chief executive through the initiative leader, project owner, and system architect to the project manager and development team member—must be able to visualize the work ahead of them. The ability to visualize an outcome *and* then to check its workability through requirements testing is vital to transformational project success.

The thinking Sam Walton used, as described in Chapter 1, to formulate his operating concept became the context within which the cross-docking project was developed. If he had not visualized the flow of goods as a continuum from raw materials through manufacturing, distributing, and retailing, that project concept would never have been conceived. His overall concept visualized how Wal-Mart and its suppliers would operate as a whole and included the way in which the total process could work, that is, with the cooperation of the manufacturers.

Although the scope and content of visual creations are different at the various points during transformational project work, the need for creative visualization and evaluation remains constant. The ability to formulate and weigh alternatives in light of constraints is the essence of creative, conceptual system thinking required to find superior, workable solutions.

What happens when the combination of creative, conceptual thinking and constructive analysis within the context of accountability is either shortcut or bypassed completely? Doing so can cause major problems. Documented, workable operating and project concepts, crucial to effective project execution, are missing. Potential transformational projects that could dramatically improve the way cross-boundary work is accomplished are likely to be pulled apart by conflicting requirements of the individual user areas because overall concepts do not exist. Projects fail because workability, an integral part of concept creation, is not considered a determining factor in the operating and project conceptual designs.

System Workability

The entire Transformational Project Paradigm (TPP) initiative process, from the development and clarification by senior management of the strategic direction through project concepts implemented by the project development team, *must consider workability as a necessity.* The TPP initiative leader, project owners, system architects, and functional managers must meld their expertise into a coordinated source of useful information from which innovative and workable operating and project concepts can flow. Operating and project concept formulation is a combination of seeing the whole, interweaving the relevant details, and testing the concepts against constraints and requirements to assure workability.

System architects must be satisfied that their designs will meet requirements through advanced information technology techniques before proposing an operating or project concept to the TPP initiative leader or to a project owner. Peter Senge, a leading authority in systems thinking and organizational learning, comments on the relationship of workability to design by stating: "Design is, by its nature, an integrative science because *design requires making something work in practice.*"[2]

The TPP initiative leader and project owners, in turn, must understand how the operating and related project concepts will work to fulfill the TPP initiative goals and objectives. They must be held accountable for workable proposals submitted to senior management for consideration and approval.

The development path recommendation (custom design and programming, specific application package(s), or a combination of both) is deferred under the TPP until project concept time to increase the probability that the choice will work in practice. Detailed user requirements testing performed at that time can prevent later unpleasant surprises.

Creating the Operating Concept

The strategic TPP initiative, described in general terms, *must be expanded and structured by means of the operating concept* to provide the basis for breaking out manageable segments, the project concepts. In this way the actual projects will tie to the fulfillment of the TPP initiative goals and objectives through the *bridge of the operating concept.* Without this bridge, projects that are unlikely to fulfill the intent of the strategic initiative will be formulated and carried out, wasting valuable time and resources.

Understanding the Problem

Understanding the problem goes well beyond comprehending the goals and objectives of the TPP initiative. It includes knowing the *specifics* about how related work is done and the constraints that must be taken into account for a target solution. In-depth understanding of TPP initiative goals and objectives, business area practices, advanced information technology techniques, and business and technical constraints gives the master system architect and other key participants an appreciation of the total problem to be solved. As John Dewey said: "A problem well stated is half solved."[3]

Operating Concept as the Key Link

The goals and objectives defined by senior management for a strategic TPP initiative have adequate detail for management understanding. The Price Waterhouse survey mentioned earlier, however, found a major difficulty with the entirely different level of detail presented by the corporate plan compared to that needed for systems development.[4] A master system architect assisted by process area system architects, and in cooperation with the other TPP initiative principals, must expand upon the level of detail in the TPP initiative goals and objectives in order to:

- clarify the extent and nature of problem to be solved
- delineate scope
- formulate alternative target solutions supported by advanced information technology
- test the target solutions against constraints and business area requirements
- prepare the proposal for the recommended alternative
- present the proposal, through the TPP initiative leader, to senior management and the board of directors for approval.

The proposed operating concept must show the TPP initiative goals and objectives in sufficient documented detail to permit breakout of project concepts, which, in turn, will define the project execution that will realize the stated business objectives. Thus, the operating concept becomes *the key link* between the TPP initiative goals and objectives and the results realized through transformational project implementation.

Defining the Scope

Operating concept application areas follow a *natural scope* that encompasses all of the current and future tasks necessary to produce the intended overall result. The natural scope becomes clearer as conceptual work proceeds. Premature setting of scope through arbitrary decisions can upset the entire process by forcing an incorrect boundary on the work that must be performed to achieve the initiative goals and objectives.

Since scope is a primary determinant of work effort, the architects must be allowed to study boundaries as part of the conceptual work, rather than having the Transformational Project Paradigm (TPP) initiative leader and project owners encounter the need for scope redefinition and probable expansion later during the development phase of the projects. Uncontrolled *scope creep* causes delay and added costs, at a minimum. It can cause the need to reconceptualize the operating concept, which, if ignored, can be a source of initiative failure.

The master system architect delineates the operating concept boundary (scope) based on the flow of work involved in meeting current and future goals and objectives. For example, a supply chain optimization initiative for a manufacturer would encompass raw material acquisition from suppliers through delivery of finished goods to customers. The master system architect should work with specialized system architects and functional managers to define projects within the operating concept, for instance, raw materials acquisition, production control, and finished goods distribution.

Seldom is there a clear line of demarcation between one application area and another. A business work area rarely is independent because tasks and actions go beyond it. The system architects must evaluate the best boundaries for the operating and project concepts, taking functional accountabilities and the extent of data and communication relationships into account. Project concept detailing work will proceed later, *after* approval of the operating concept.

The Need for System Architect Immersion in the Subject Matter

System architects must have access to all business areas within the operating concept scope and must be able to communicate effectively with contributors in these units. The goal is to formulate an operating concept that meets each unit's specific requirements while making significant improvement in work performance to benefit the company.

System architects must immerse themselves in the subject matter. They must know *in detail* how the business areas reach their objectives and how such work can be adapted to fulfill continuing mandatory and desired objectives in support of the strategic direction. Briefings held with users to obtain explanations of business practices are not enough to provide the degree of immersion necessary to formulate recommended, workable solution alternatives.

In addition, the system architect must learn what other companies are doing in concept-related areas, meet with representatives of leading software package vendors to understand techniques and trends, and obtain and read reference material about the subject areas. System architects must have the ability to conceive workable models by considering business aspects from various perspectives. All of this work must occur within the guidelines of the TPP initiative goals and objectives to avoid random collection of unrelated, massive detail. A creativity researcher notes two reasons for immersion: "It may be that immersion in our subject matter is a condition of creative thinking not only because it gives us material with which to think but also because it acquaints us with the difficulties of the problem."[5] Immersion in the subject matter, without preconceived ideas, allows system architects to objectively assimilate data that can become a basis for evaluating and formulating the operating concept.

Formulating Target Solutions and Researching Development Options

At this point in the process the master system architect should solicit ideas from *all sources* for consideration, evaluation, and possible incorporation into the operating concept. Proposed ideas need to be examined through *constructive, analytical thinking* to determine whether the contributions are realistic and workable from the business and technological points of view. This step focuses on the *feasible* ideas for inclusion in the operating concepts.

The master system architect formulates alternative target solutions that will meet the Transformational Project Paradigm (TPP) initiative goals and objectives in cooperation with key personnel. Parts of the tentative solutions will come from many sources including contributions by interested groups and committees. The TPP initiative leader and business managers can provide guidance on the concept. System architects from each major process area in the company will suggest how advanced information technology can be deployed to improve operations for their respective areas. The chief information officer and system concepts department manager should contribute ideas and sound practices based on their background and experience.

If application packages are viable options, the master system architect should ask selected vendors to provide preliminary proposals outlining an approach to the application areas, a general cost estimate, and a list of installations at other companies. After approval of the operating concept, detailed review and recommendation for a specific choice is part of project conceptual work.

How does conceptual thinking take place to develop the target solution? Researchers have found that professional system designers perform the following mental processes at lightning speed:

1. They mentally constructed a model of a proposed solution to the problem.
2. They mentally executed the model—in essence, running a simulation on the model—to see if it solved the problem.
3. When they found that it didn't (usually because it was too simple), they played the inadequate model back against those parts of the problem to see where it failed and then enhanced the model in those areas.
4. They repeated steps 1–3 until they had a model that appeared to solve the problem.[6]

Continuing focus is necessary for creating a superior operating concept to meet the goals and objectives of the TPP initiative. To accomplish this, it is crucial to generate alternative concepts and to evaluate them objectively before proposing the specific operating concept.

Preparing, Evaluating, and Approving the Proposal

The master system architect prepares the operating concept proposal in cooperation with the system architects for the specialized processes and with counsel from the other TPP initiative principals. The group selects the best operating concept alternative to recommend after weighing each possibility. At a minimum, the proposal should include the following information:

- recommendation for meeting the TPP initiative goals and objectives with the operating concept
- effect of the operating concept on organizational structure and on management responsibilities
- evaluation of system stability in the target area and overall readiness to embark on the initiative
- plan for transition of affected user personnel
- degree of conformity with the technical infrastructure
- effect on current and fixed assets
- resource requirements
- cost estimate range for funding
- justification for the recommended alternative using the most likely development path
- estimated timeline range
- potential issues and problems
- synopsis of other alternatives and their shortcomings.

The goal is to obtain *mutual understanding* with senior management, and among all involved, of how the recommended operating concept will support the TPP initiative, given effective project concept formulation and execution.

Adjustments to the Operating Concept

The need for adjustments *will* arise after the operating concept proposal is approved and project work is initiated. At times it may even be necessary to recast the operating concept when changes in circumstances— perhaps in the marketplace, in the field of advanced information technology, or as new learning occurs—come about as work is proceeding. Senior management should recognize that there are likely to be changes *unknown at the outset* that can affect the overall direction of project work.

The TPP initiative leader is responsible for *keeping the operating concept geared to the TPP initiative goals and objectives.* The TPP initiative leader must maintain the operating concept as a viable bridge between the initiative and the actual changes that will be brought about through transformational project implementation. She remains responsible for the operating concept until it is fully implemented through execution of all related projects. Only the TPP initiative leader, therefore, should have authority to approve changes to the operating concept after proposal approval.

Creating the Project Concepts

The master system architect makes a rough cut of the individual project boundaries after management has approved the operating concept. The system concepts manager appoints system architects, preferably the same ones who worked with the master system architect to prepare the operating concept proposal, to formulate the project concepts. These system architects report on a project basis to project owners appointed by the Transformational Project Paradigm (TPP) initiative leader.

The project concepts form workable target solutions for system development. Each project concept, when approved in documented proposal form, becomes the basis for an actual project, or work segment, of the operating concept. If possible, the project managers should be available to work with the system architects on project proposal preparation to facilitate coordination at turnover time.

The project concept defines how the business objectives for the project will be accomplished, consistent with the operating concept design. The relationship between a project concept and its business objectives is comparable to the relationship between the operating concept and its TPP initiative goals and objectives. These two sets of relationships are necessary to form a direct but flexible link between the strategic direction and related advanced information technology deployment.

The need for changes and adjustments in user personnel often arises while conceiving and developing a new project. Careful planning by the project owner can minimize turmoil for everyone. Determining who will be affected and retraining in transferable job skills and eventual reassignment can avoid abrupt job loss that is cruel and unnecessary. The project owner should draw from information in the early conceptual design to advise affected user personnel on anticipated changes so that they will have time to take appropriate action to make the transition.

Ideally, project owners and system architects will participate from the outset in operating concept formulation. In any event, they will need to have sufficient information to ensure alignment of the project concepts with the operating concept.

Much has been written about defining a project for subsequent development. Regardless of the approach chosen to formulate a project concept, the seven interrelated steps listed below are crucial for transformational project work:

1. Understand the problem.
2. Define the scope.
3. Formulate target solutions.
4. Adapt the solutions to fulfill user requirements.
5. Choose the development path.
6. Prepare and approve the project proposal.
7. Structure the project.

The work in the first six steps is performed in greater detail than that described in Creating the Operating Concept. Steps 4, 5, 6, and 7 examine project concept differences.

Adapt the Solutions to Fulfill User Requirements

The requirements testing step in the project conceptual process should determine if a target solution *will meet real needs of the users*. At this point, requirements specified by business managers and staff members who will be using the system must be tested against the proposed target solutions using the *constructive, analytical* mode of thinking. The project owner has the final authority to determine which target solution, adapted as needed, best meets the necessary requirements. If the system architect finds that the selected alternative is technically feasible, she will proceed in leading work on the design document for the project concept.

The conceptual design documents for the project concepts, in final form, describe how the proposed systems will work. They contain an overview, narrative task descriptions, data flow diagrams, primary data elements, transaction volumes, and related information. The documents must contain enough detail to allow final evaluation in respect to workability.

Choose the Development Path

Based on design documents for the project concepts, system architects investigate the potential development paths of cross-functional integrated packages, functional area packages, and custom development. If vendor-supplied packages are indicated, the decision to choose an integrated or functional package approach must be evaluated carefully by the master and process area system architects, project owners, the TPP initiative leader, and the chief information officer.

Functional packages usually meet more user requirements than integrated packages but may lack sophisticated technical integration between functional areas. The TPP initiative leader, in consultation with the chief information officer, must have the authority to make the final decision on the integrated versus functional package path because he is responsible for the success or failure of the initiative.

Consequently, the TPP initiative leader has the power to choose a specific integrated package or to pursue integrated custom development for the same reason. If an integrated package or overall custom development path is not indicated, individual project owners can choose functional packages or custom development for their areas because the owners are accountable for success or failure of their projects.

An integrated or functional package approach can have ramifications on the technical infrastructure that must be considered as part of the overall decision. If infrastructure changes are indicated, the TPP initiative leader and project owners will need to negotiate the advisability of making such changes with the chief information officer, considering tradeoffs among functionality, package integration, and the technical infrastructure. If negotiations between these initiative principals do not produce an agreed-upon result, the principals should follow the review policy established by senior management.

Prepare and Approve the Project Proposal

The system architect, under direction of the project owner, prepares the project proposal after the specific development path has been selected. The chief information officer finalizes the related document, showing the cost and timing of any changes in the infrastructure required by the proposed system, for review and approval by senior management. If the project proposal is consistent with the operating concept, the Transformational Project Paradigm (TPP) initiative leader approves it subject to funding policy established by the company. If the project proposal requires a change in the operating concept, affecting the TPP initiative goals and objectives, the initiative leader must consult with the chief executive and chief operating officer. In all cases projects must be consistent with the original or revised operating concept because the projects are the means to realize the goals and objectives of the strategic TPP initiative.

Specific project proposal contents are similar to those of the operating concept proposal but are shown below for clarification:

- explanation of relevance between the recommended project concept and the related business objectives and user requirements
- effect of the project concept on organizational structure and on management responsibilities

- evaluation of existing system stability for the business area and its readiness to embark on the project
- plan for transition of affected user personnel
- degree of conformity with the technical infrastructure
- effect on current or fixed assets
- resource requirements
- cost estimate range for budgeting purposes
- justification for the recommended alternative including the specific development path
- estimated timeline range
- potential issues and problems
- synopsis of other alternatives and their shortcomings.

Upon approval of the project proposal, the system architect structures the project in cooperation with the assigned project manager.

Structure the Project

The project manager must gain an in-depth understanding of project business objectives and how the project concept addresses them. The manager must feel comfortable in his level of knowledge about the subject matter to lead project execution without wondering if all the objectives will be met.

At the point of turnover, the system architect and project manager review together the specifics about data flow, system interfaces, user requirements, and other related design items. Based on their cooperative work, the turnover documents should include the project concept documents, proposal, and the initial project plan prepared by the project manager, with counsel from the system architect.

The project manager must have the authority to *refuse acceptance* of a project concept and development path *without recrimination* if her analysis at turnover time determines that the direction is not feasible. The project manager, in making this decision, must be equal in status with the system architect under the project owner. By having the authority to refuse to proceed based on the facts of the situation and on project execution experience, project failure can be avoided before development work starts. Of course, refusal would be the last resort of a project manager and would only occur in the unlikely event that the system architect, project manager, and project owner cannot work out an acceptable concept and development path.

The chief information officer should define a complete set of turnover documents required as part of the system development guidelines. The project owner must approve the turnover, including the fact that all required documents have been completed. It is crucial that the project owner is satisfied that the project manager has gained the degree of understanding necessary to carry the project forward successfully.

8

Project Execution Focus

Leadership involves creating a vision that draws people forward toward a common desired reality. The corporate vision is focused on a goal, and this helps create a unified focus for everyone. Focus is one of the reasons why use of vision increases productivity.

James A. Ritscher, in *Transforming Leadership*

Much excellent information is available on project execution in the form of written material and courses. Rather than attempt to summarize it, I want to stress one attribute—focus—that is essential to successful execution.

Project execution demands that *variables be held to a minimum*. Failure to do so can cause project failure on otherwise well-managed projects. A project manager always will have unforeseen demands to confront *without outside variables* because systems development is a learning experience where more and more becomes known as team members delve into greater detail. *Focus* means that a project manager must concentrate on solving problems that are under his control without being sidetracked by issues that are actually the accountability of others. Such issues can cause upsets in project execution, which unfairly fall upon the project manager.

Every large information systems project has many variables that must be addressed directly by the project manager. Examples of these include: previously unidentified and/or unforeseen requirements, changes in scope to accommodate data paths as interfaces are further defined, program size and performance problems, and unplanned personnel changes.

These represent only a few of the many issues that surface during system development. The project owner must assess variables as they arise to differentiate those that are the direct responsibility of the project manager from those that affect the project but are the responsibility of others who must handle them within the accountability framework of the Transformational Project Paradigm. If neglected, these outside variables can be left to the project manager by default causing upsets, delays, and extra cost.

Major Actions Needed for Transformational Project Execution

Focus does not mean that the project manager should be unaware of trends, ideas, and conditions that can affect the course of the project. In fact, the project manager and owner must seek and evaluate constructive ideas and comments from all participants, both individually and in groups, including development team members, key users, technical specialists, and the project management department manager. This input can provide important background for actions that the project manager must focus on, with project owner support. The major ones include:

- splitting the defined overall project into interrelated subprojects
- choosing an implementation strategy
- drafting a work breakdown structure
- utilizing version control (configuration management)
- scheduling work, assigning tasks, and monitoring progress
- formulating the data conversion plan and developing the conversion subsystem
- structuring the test plan and reviewing test results
- deciding on system cutover to production status.

Splitting the Defined Project into Interrelated Subprojects

Transformational project development can take two or more years. When possible, it is highly advantageous for management control purposes, and for continuing support of the project, to split the defined project into *interrelated* subprojects that can be implemented in about six-month intervals.

Although the need to split a large project into six-month segments has been recommended many times, it often is unclear that succeeding subprojects must build upon the ones implemented earlier, fulfilling the total project concept. Indeed, implementing a roughly defined subproject merely to meet the six-month guideline can extend and make more costly total project execution because excessive rework becomes necessary before the next subproject can start. Unfortunately, some projects do *not* lend themselves to being split because the application segments are so tightly integrated.

Nadler and Hibino have found in their research of leading problem solvers that when a project is split into subprojects, each new product or system must become the stepping stone to the next. This observation, which they call the *solution-after-next* principle, calls for an immediate solution (a subproject) to be a transitional step toward a better future (successful project completion).[1]

Choosing an Implementation Strategy

Implementation strategy concerns the manner in which the system will be deployed. Choices include pilot operation of the full system cycle in a small division or unit of the company, implementation of part of the system in either one business unit or across units, or a variation of these two basic approaches. Implementation strategy must be considered when deciding how to split a project into subprojects because the two basic choices require different development sequences.

Drafting a Work Breakdown Structure

The work breakdown structure (WBS), originated by the United States Department of Defense as a contractor requirement for defining large and complex projects, is a graphical chart in levels of detail that shows the end products to be developed for each system component. The project manager uses the WBS for a project or subproject to: define scope; set up sufficiently small subdivisions for estimating, personnel assignment, and detailed visibility; and serve as the chart of accounts against which estimates and costs are recorded. The work breakdown structure is a key document that the project manager must maintain and use to keep control of the project and related subprojects.

Utilizing Version Control (Configuration Management)

Version control, as it is called in software development, serves the same purpose that configuration management performs in manufacturing, for example, in aircraft production. In each case, a defined portion of the product is managed under tight change and accounting control procedures. Software development demands a decision point when changes to a component must be restricted to a bare minimum by the project owner. Failure to have a sound version control procedure forces programmers to work toward a moving target which can cause lost time, rework, and overruns.

Software development version control supplements project owner management control over changes. A software package keeps track of changes in programs to avoid confusion between programmers who work on related parts of programs. Although this kind of tool can help avoid confusion and costly delays, it must be used to support management control for maximum effectiveness in outcome.

Scheduling Work, Assigning Tasks, and Monitoring Progress

The project manager must schedule work in the sequence necessary to produce the individual software products while dealing with time and resource constraints. To achieve project success, she must evaluate and use estimates from the development team members as input to scheduling and personnel loading.

Often, a large gap exists between management expectations of when a software product can be produced and time estimates from the development team members. This gap constitutes one of the most difficult challenges for a project manager who is caught between what actually can be accomplished and what management unrealistically expects.

The Transformational Project Paradigm, in holding the project owner accountable for project success or failure, supports realistic scheduling. Development staff must work under realistic expectations to achieve desired results. Staff members have little motivation to excel when they anticipate being judged as failures in terms of missed schedules, regardless of how much they produce.

Formulating the Data Conversion Plan and Developing the Subsystem

Every new system requires conversion of data from existing systems and possibly from manual records. Transformational projects often require data from separate, dissimilar systems. Determining how this disparate data can be converted into a reliable form can be a daunting task.

The conversion plan must be defined as a separate subproject requiring definition, specification, and development of a conversion subsystem. Thorough testing and operation of this subsystem must be done before any of the application subsystems are installed. Failure to give conversion planning and the subsystem the attention and resources they deserve can produce an inaccurate, incomplete initial database. In the worst case, it can cause the entire implementation to be redone at considerable cost and delay.

Structuring the Test Plan and Reviewing Test Results

A well-conceived, thorough software test plan is essential for a transformational project because the system affects mainstream operations. Successful analytical testing progresses in increments; expansion of breadth depends upon the thoroughness and results of the prior steps. Accountability for each step should be placed with an individual who determines the readiness of work under his control for the next testing step.

The project manager is accountable for the readiness of a system for user acceptance testing. The project owner, based on the recommendations of the project manager and user managers, is accountable for making the decision for the system to go into live production. These principles hold for any testing process. Starting complete system cycle testing earlier through *builds* is gaining favor over earlier techniques that left complete system testing for the later stages.

Deciding on Cutover to Production Status

The project owner is accountable for making the decision to place the new system into production status. To improve the probability that the new system will balance with required controls, the project owner should decide whether parallel operation with the old system(s) is in order. Although parallel operation is a desirable safeguard, it may be infeasible because the new system(s) is not comparable in its functions with the existing system(s).

The project manager and owner will need to formulate an alternative user acceptance testing approach if parallel testing is not feasible. Alternatives can include performing more in-depth testing, selecting representative portions of the system for balancing review, and assigning selected user personnel for de facto production testing.

As an integral part of the decision for the system to go into live production, the project owner must be satisfied with the readiness of user managers and staff to handle new or revised job assignments, development and career planning for personnel who will be adversely affected by the change, and coordination of the effects on current and fixed assets.

Project Execution Issues and Problems

A Transformational Project Paradigm (TPP) initiative can be supportive of a company's strategic direction, and then the competitive marketplace can change, seemingly on the next day, causing the need to revise strategy. Many potential changes in strategic direction, however, do not happen quickly and can be foreseen. Senior management should anticipate changes that might occur and assign a probability to each of them. By doing this, the TPP initiative leader, knowing the likelihood of changes, can make informed decisions.

Every transformational project will have issues and problems that need addressing as work proceeds, even though TPP initiative goals and objectives are still consistent with the company's strategic direction. The project owner and project manager must evaluate, before starting project execution work, *major variables* and take action either to *prevent their harmful effects* or, if that is not possible, to *provide for the effects in the project plan* by notifying the TPP initiative leader of their potential impact. Once work has begun, all expect the project to proceed within a reasonable schedule. These major variables include:

- project feasibility
- infrastructure changes
- standards and development guidelines changes
- priority issues
- maintaining accountability
- technical and user area stability
- readiness for and acceptance of the management reporting system
- lateral coordination capability
- established communication plan.

Project Feasibility

Circumstances may change after the system architect completes the project conceptual work and cooperates with the project manager in the turnover approved by the project owner. Before starting project execution work, the project manager must again review the feasibility of accomplishing the project within the proposed time schedule and cost range. This review should encompass conditions necessary for a successful project including availability of an adequate number of development team staff members with the required skills; availability or planned acquisition of all technical components including computing capacity, storage, networking, and database and operating system software; and review of the recommended software package(s), if any, to see whether it still remains the best choice and has a high probability of working in the user and technical environments.

Even though the project manager has previously agreed with the system architect and project owner at turnover time to proceed with the project, the project manager must have the authority to recommend subsequent changes to the project owner. As a last resort, the project manager must maintain the authority at this time to refuse the project without recrimination. Proceeding with an unsound project invites failure.

Infrastructure Changes

The chief information officer is responsible for the infrastructure used by transformational projects and therefore is authorized to determine it, but she negotiates changes with the TPP initiative leader and project owners. Choosing and implementing the right infrastructure for the company is a challenging task for the chief information officer. Infrastructure choices—computers, networking, operating systems, database access systems, and common application programs—are constantly evolving as technology advances. Since application projects are always in progress, an infrastructure change cannot be implemented without affecting the progress of one or more projects.

Ideally, a transformational project can be initiated with the infrastructure that will continue through system cutover. If this cannot be done, the project manager must be given the flexibility to add the rework effect on the project schedule and cost ranges to the project plan.

Standards and Development Guidelines Changes

A change in standards or development guidelines has a less severe effect on a transformational project than a change in infrastructure. Even so, project personnel need to take time to learn the new material, and possibly to revise documentation prepared. The learning time and related diversion from the project can break the flow of work, thereby slowing the project. If the chief information officer finds it necessary to change the standards or development guidelines during the course of a transformational project, the project manager should set up the change as a separate set of tasks outside those directly related to the project.

Priority Issues

The Transformational Project Paradigm (TPP) initiative leader and project owners must ascertain the likelihood that existing or planned initiatives will affect resources needed for the transformational project. The TPP initiative leader *must establish continuing priority with senior management* for the transformational projects associated with the initiative to avoid delays, rework, and possible failure caused by the unpredictability of resources. Successful transformational projects *demand a long-term commitment* by dedicated, competent individuals during the time that their skills are required for project progress.

Maintaining Accountability

The beginning-to-end accountability structure described in Chapter 4 needs to be maintained as project execution takes place. Every step along the continuum can be questioned as project execution proceeds because more becomes known about the entire TPP initiative as programs are defined and developed. The overall initiative therefore remains active, albeit to a lesser extent, until all systems go into live production.

Technical and User Area Stability

Project owners and project managers must assess existing systems, procedures, and the working environment to see that existing systems are technically sound enough to continue operating during the transformational project without requiring emergency attention and that user personnel who are required to participate in the project can, in fact, spend sufficient time on those duties without jeopardizing the requirements of their existing jobs.

Transformational projects can suffer a de facto loss of priority from demands of existing systems and from current work in the user areas if the required participants are faced with unrealistic demands. Time loss can be insidious. Small losses disappear from the project because of user staff members' inability to keep appointments, provide information, and concentrate on the project even when they are physically present during project activities. As Frederick Brooks recites: "How does a project get to be a year late? ... One day at a time."[2]

Readiness for and Acceptance of the Management Reporting System

Accountability becomes real when the related reporting system is in place to report performance and costs to each manager in the TPP continuum. The reporting system, discussed in Chapter 6, displays personnel commitments, estimates, and actual costs to all interested parties. The personnel commitments, in particular, relate to the ability of the project manager to make available the required team members with appropriate skills when needed. The reporting system needs to be in place, used, and accepted by the chief information officer, TPP initiative leader, and project owners.

Lateral Coordination Capability

The ability for companies to succeed in cross-lateral coordination is much easier during planning and conceptual work than when actual changes in work content, responsibility, and authority begin to take place. Company personnel who participate in planning and design sessions often wonder if the implementation *will* take place. Even if it does, they think such changes either will not occur in full or will be done at a distant date.

When transformational projects begin, reluctance to proceed from those who will be adversely affected can diminish the success of the effort. To minimize resistance and maximize the alignment and motivation necessary to make the project a success, the TPP initiative leader and project owners must work with affected personnel in advance and as implementation begins. They must alleviate fears of adversely affected personnel by arranging for retraining and reassignment when possible.

Established Communication Plan

The Transformational Project Paradigm (TPP) initiative leader, project owners, project managers, and staff members should receive progress reports in appropriate levels of detail. In addition, other communication means, such as regular progress and milestone meetings, need to be scheduled to brief management and project participants about progress, issues, and problems. A sound communication plan furnishes all interested parties with the degree of project visibility appropriate to their responsibilities. Such visibility can reduce unpleasant surprises, while giving the TPP initiative leader, project owners, and project managers an opportunity to cite individual and team accomplishments.

Successful management of these major variables will enhance the probability of successful execution. Responsibility for each variable must be established *before* the project starts and continue *throughout* the life of the project.

9

Taking Responsibility

What does responsibility mean? Responsibility means not blaming anyone or anything for your situation, including yourself. Having accepted this circumstance, this event, this problem, responsibility then means the ability to have a creative response to the situation as it is now. All problems contain the seeds of opportunity, and this awareness allows you to take the moment and transform it to a better situation or thing.

Deepak Chopra, *The Seven Spiritual Laws of Success*

The Transformational Project Paradigm (TPP) is a framework, which, when customized in detail for a company, becomes the context for effective deployment of advanced information technology. Clarity of purpose, acknowledgment of good work, career progression based on accomplishment, objective evaluation of ideas and proposals, and earned trust and confidence among all participants are all vital aspects of the TPP. Innovative staff contributions by trained and qualified personnel are nurtured when loyalty, trust, and compassion are present to foster *creative, conceptual thinking.*

Creative, conceptual thinking generates target solutions—the operating and project concepts—in the TPP. The target solutions are then evaluated by means of *constructive analysis,* through requirements testing, to see that the solutions will meet real needs. *Both* creative, conceptual thinking and constructive analysis are required to formulate workable concepts for successful deployment of advanced information technology through transformational project execution.

The TPP addresses issues involved in deployment of advanced information technology for business-critical, cross-boundary systems—only. (Issues relating to choices made by senior management for the strategic direction, business organizational structure and practices, administration of business operations, and information technology infrastructure are among topics that are beyond the scope of this book.) The TPP is a structure that can be utilized in the deployment of advanced information technology regardless of a company's organizational structure—consolidated corporate with overall functions, separate business units, centralized or decentralized operations, or other variations. Similarly, the TPP is applicable to any combination of providing information systems technical personnel—in-house, consultant/contractor, or outsourcing arrangement—and also to any combination of technical architecture including mainframe, client/server, and network-centric. When the TPP framework is customized specifically for a company, senior management can deploy advanced information technology creatively with a high probability of success.

Customizing the Transformational Project Paradigm Framework for Transformational Project Work

Initially, the chief executive-led senior management team will need to consider a number of company-specific issues in customizing the TPP. These might include: decisions to locate the system concepts, project management, and development resource pool departments at corporate or business-unit level; the extent of outsourcing to be employed for the three departments; and assessment of the company's ability to operate successfully in a cross-lateral organizational mode. The objective is to identify and decide on *any issues* that would affect viability of the customized TPP.

Senior management should then be ready to set up the customized, detailed context within which transformational project work can take place. To accomplish this, management needs to establish relevant TPP policies, responsibilities, and performance measurements:

- Define personnel policies supportive of reaching the maximum potential of advanced information technology and considerate of employee desires for stability and career growth (Chapters 3, 4, and 5).
- Establish a structure within the information systems division containing system concepts, project management, and development resource pool home departments with appointment of department managers for each (Chapter 5).
- Define specific roles and responsibilities for the board of directors, for the chief executive-led senior management team including the chief information officer, and for the TPP initiative principals: Transformational Project Paradigm (TPP) initiative leader, project owner, master system architect, system architect, and project manager (Chapter 4).
- Establish enabling policies for TPP initiative matrix management (Chapter 5).
- Organize a forum for groups and committees, which allows their ideas and suggestions to be offered within a setting of accountability (Chapters 4 and 7).
- Formulate justification guidelines that are appropriate for TPP initiative/project goals and objectives (Chapter 7).
- Specify and implement a TPP initiative management reporting system (Chapter 6).
- Establish management responsibility for review and decision-making to resolve conflicts in resources that may arise during transformational project work (Chapters 7 and 8).
- Establish a management review procedure to resolve infrastructure issues that cannot be negotiated successfully by the chief information officer and the TPP user principals (Chapter 5).

Customizing and detailing the TPP will require a considerable amount of work by management, information systems division, and user representatives. A senior executive should be placed in charge of the overall project to establish the TPP management practices context for advanced information technology deployment.

Context Benefits

The management practices context, based on the nature of systems work, should provide a solid foundation for TPP initiatives to proceed toward optimal deployment of advanced information technology. Benefits can include:

- clarity in performance at all levels
- alignment of advanced information technology deployment with the strategic direction
- new opportunities from dramatic improvement in the way work is performed
- stabilization of the system development process
- advanced information technology deployment with a minimum of disruption in ongoing operations
- reduced turnover of and better growth opportunities for information systems division management and project team personnel
- competitive value from superior, workable concepts that are executed effectively
- higher probability of implementation success for business critical, cross-boundary systems.

Facilitating Transformational Project Work

The chief executive-led senior management team can facilitate transformational project work by establishing an environment with fairly placed accountability that supports cross-boundary coordination, creativity, and constructive analysis at all levels. This nurturing environment can provide opportunities for people to achieve significant results for the company because it is consistent with the nature of systems work. The TPP initiative leader is accountable for coordination of day-to-day TPP activities, keeping senior management fully informed about ongoing progress, and success of advanced information technology deployment for his initiative. This leader must have the support and continuing, informed attention of the chief executive-led senior management team.

Assuming the strategic direction is on target, companies that follow the guidelines in this book can attain predictable, successful deployment of advanced information technology to increase the probability of breakthroughs in growth opportunities, productivity, cost control, capital utilization, and customer satisfaction. The TPP should help senior managers solve the underlying problems of advanced information technology deployment for business-critical systems, allowing contributors to concentrate their skills, knowledge, abilities, and energy toward achieving the promise of information technology.

Notes

Introduction

1. Pinto, Jeffrey K. 1994. *Successful Information System Implementation: The Human Side.* Upper Darby, PA: Project Management Institute, p. vi.

2. ————. 1996. *Power and Politics in Project Management.* Upper Darby, PA: Project Management Institute, p. 96.

3. Byrne, John A. 1997. Management Theory—or Fad of the Month. *Business Week* (June 23): 47.

Chapter 1: The Transformational Project Paradigm

1. de Bono, Edward. 1992. *Serious Creativity: Using the Power of Lateral Thinking to Create New Ideas.* New York: Harper Collins, p. 309.

2. O'Leary, Denis. 1997. Keep up with the Pace. *Information Week* (Sept. 22): 76.

3. Computer Sciences Corporation (CSC). 1997. *Critical Issues of Information Systems Management: 10th Annual Survey of I/S Management Issues.* El Segundo, CA, pp. 4, 7, 10, 13.

4. Prairie, Patti L. 1996. Benchmarking IT Strategic Alignment. In Jerry N. Luftman, ed. *Competing in the Information Age: Strategic Alignment in Practice.* New York: Oxford UP, p. 243.

5. Brooks, Frederick P., Jr. 1986. No Silver Bullet: Essence and Accidents of Software Engineering. In *Information Processing* 86, H.J. Kugler, ed. Amsterdam: Elsevier Science (North Holland). Reprinted as Chapter 16 in Brooks. 1995. *The Mythical Man-Month: Essays on Software Engineering.* Anniversary ed. Reading, MA: Addison-Wesley, p. 185.

6. Caldwell, Bruce. 1997. Top Execs Take IT Reins. *Information Week* (Mar. 17): 100.

7. Alter, Allan E. 1997. The Word from the Top. *Computerworld* (Dec. 15): 74.

8. Rockart, John F. 1988. The Line Takes the Leadership—IS Management in a Wired Society. *Sloan Management Review* (Summer): 57, 62.

9. Strassmann, Paul A. 1995. *The Politics of Information Management: Policy Guidelines.* New Canaan, CT: The Information Economics Press, p. 302.

10. Cleland, David I. 1994. *Project Management: Strategic Design and Implementation.* 2d ed. New York: McGraw-Hill, p. 32.

11. Hogbin, Geoff, and David V. Thomas. 1994. *Investing in Information Technology: Managing the Decision-Making Process.* London: McGraw-Hill International (UK), p. 202.

12. Katzenbach, Jon R., and Douglas K. Smith. 1994. *The Wisdom of Teams: Creating the High Performance Organization.* New York: Harper Business, pp. 268–69.

13. Fortune. 1993. Jack Welch's Lessons for Success. (Jan. 25): 88-89. Book excerpt from Tichy, Noel M., and Stratford Sherman. 1993. *Control Your Destiny or Someone Else Will.* New York: Bantam Doubleday Dell.

14. Saporito, Bill. 1992. What Sam Walton Taught America. *Fortune.* (May 4): 104.

15. Stalk, George, Philip Evans, and Lawrence E. Shulman. 1992. Competing on Capabilities: The New Rules of Corporate Strategy. *Harvard Business Review* (Mar.–Apr.): 58.

16. Ibid, 58–59.

17. Sellers, Patricia. 1992. The Dumbest Marketing Ploy. *Fortune* (Oct. 5): 88.

18. Magnet, Myron. 1994. The Productivity Payoff Arrives. *Fortune* (June 27): 82–83.

19. Katz, Robert L. 1955. Skills of an Effective Administrator. *Harvard Business Review* (Jan.–Feb.). In *People: Managing Your Most Important Asset.* Boston: Harvard Business Review, Publisher, 1992, pp. 48–49.

20. Drucker, Peter F. 1985. *Management: Tasks, Responsibilities, Practices.* New York: Harper Colophon, p. 469.

21. Nadler, Gerald, and Shozo Hibino. 1994. *Breakthrough Thinking: The Seven Principles of Creative Problem Solving.* 2d ed. Rocklin, CA: Prima Publishing, p. 35.

22. de Bono, p. 11.

23. Zaleznik, Abraham. 1989. *The Managerial Mystique: Restoring Leadership in Business.* New York: Harper & Row, p. 22.

24. DeMarco, Tom, and Timothy Lister. 1987. *Peopleware: Productive Projects and Teams.* New York: Dorset House, pp. 114-16.

Chapter 2: Moving Beyond the Current Situation

1. The Standish Group International. *Chaos.* 1994. Dennis, MA, pp. 2–7.

2. Ibid.

3. Bulkeley, William M. 1996. When Things Go Wrong. *The Wall Street Journal,* technology supplement. (Nov. 18); and King, Julia. 1997. IS Reins in Runaway Projects. *Computerworld* (Feb. 24): 1.

4. Maglitta, Joseph E. 1995. Anxious Allies. *Computerworld* Special Report. (June 12): 5–9.

5. Ibid., p. 6.

6. Ibid., p. 5.

7. *Fortune.* 1997. Fortune 500 Ranked by Performance (Apr. 28): F-28.

8. Ewusi-Mensah, Kweku. 1997. Critical Issues in Abandoned Information Systems Development Projects. *Communications of the ACM* (Sept.): 75–76.

9. Information Technology Association of America. 1998. *Help Wanted: A Call for Collaborative Action for the New Millenium.* Arlington, VA (Jan. 12): 3, 7.

10. Garner, Rochelle, and David Weldon. 1998. The Numbers Game. *Computerworld* (Jan. 26): 89.

11. Melymuka, Kathleen. 1997. We're in the Money. *Computerworld* (Sept. 1): 62.

12. Garner, Rochelle, and David Weldon. 1998. The Numbers Game. *Computerworld* (Jan. 26): 89; and Garner, Rochelle. 1998. Pressure Gap: Transforming the IT Workforce. *Computerworld* (Feb. 2): 76.

13. Garner, Rochelle, and David Weldon. 1998. The Numbers Game. *Computerworld* (Jan. 26): 89.

14. Williamson, Miryam. 1998. Quarterly Hiring Outlook: No Day at the Beach. *Computerworld* (Apr. 6): 84–85.

15. Clark, Charles E., et al. 1997. Building Change-Readiness Capabilities in the IS Organization: Insights from the Bell Atlantic Experience. *MIS Quarterly* (Dec. 1997): 427, 430, 432.

16. Brooks, Frederick P., Jr. 1995. *The Mythical Man-Month: Essays on Software Engineering.* Anniversary ed. Reading, MA: Addison-Wesley, p. 255.

17. Quoted in LaPlante, Alice.1995. Scope Grope. *Computerworld* (Mar. 20): 81.

18. McConnell, Steve. 1996. *Rapid Development: Taming Wild Software Schedules.* Redmond, WA: Microsoft Press, pp. 168, 197.

19. Kiewel, Brad. 1998. Measuring Progress in Software Development. *PM Network* (Jan.): 32.

20. Gause, Donald C., and Gerald M. Weinberg. 1989. *Exploring Requirements: Quality before Design.* New York: Dorset House, p. 277.

21. McConnell, p. 47.

22. King, Julia. 1997. IS Reins in Runaway Projects. *Computerworld* (Feb. 24): 16, and presentation slide with note from The Standish Group International.

23. Brooks. 1986. No Silver Bullet reprint, p. 186.

24. Archibald, Russell D. 1992. *Managing High-Technology Programs and Projects.* 2d ed. New York: John Wiley, p. 10.

25. Cash, James I., F. Warren McFarland, and James L. McKenney. 1992. *Corporate Information Systems Management: The Issues Facing Senior Executives.* 3d ed. Homewood, IL: Business One Irwin, p. 9.

26. Archibald. 1993. Re-Tooling the Project-Driven Organization. *PM Network* (Nov.): 7.

27. Nadler and Hibino, p. 97.

28. Gates, Bill, with Nathan Myhrvold and Peter Rinearson. 1996. *The Road Ahead.* Rev. ed. New York: Viking Penguin, p. 157.

Chapter 3: Reorganization as a Change Lever

1. Katzenbach, Jon R., and Douglas K. Smith, p. 256.

2. Arthur D. Little. 1994. *Managing Organizational Change: How Leading Organizations Are Meeting the Challenge.* Cambridge, MA: pp. 4, 13.

3. Lipnack, Jessica, and Jeffrey Stamps. 1994. *The Age of the Network: Organizing Principles for the 21st Century.* Essex Junction, VT: Oliver Wight Publications, p. 143.

4. Miles, Raymond E., and Charles C. Snow. 1994. *Fit, Failure, and the Hall of Fame: How Companies Succeed or Fail.* New York: The Free Press/Macmillan, pp. 145–47.

5. *CalBusiness.* 1997. New Center Focuses on Innovations in Organizational Effectiveness. (Fall): 7.

6. Rockart, John F., and James E. Short. 1989. IT in the 1990s: Managing Organizational Interdependence. *Sloan Management Review* (Winter): 7.

7. Ibid.

8. Cash, James I., Jr. 1996. The Bottom of Your List. *Information Week* (Mar. 25): 132.

9. Cleland. pp. 238, 240–245.

10. Applegate, Lynda M., James I. Cash, Jr., and D. Quinn Mills. 1988. Information Technology and Tomorrow's Manager. *Harvard Business Review* (Nov.–Dec.): 129.

11. Chilton, Kenneth, and Murray Weidenbaum. 1994. *A New Social Contract for the American Workplace: From Paternalism to Partnering.* St. Louis: Center for the Study of American Business (Nov.): 13.

12. Wysocki, Bernard, Jr. 1995. Lean—and Frail Some Companies Cut Costs Too Far, Suffer Corporate "Anorexia." *The Wall Street Journal* (July 5).

13. Garvin, David A. 1995. Beyond Total Quality Management and Reengineering: Managing through Processes. Commentary by author in Leveraging Processes for Strategic Advantage: A Roundtable with Xerox's Allaire, USAA's Herres, SmithKline Beecham's Leschley, and Pepsi's Weatherup. *Harvard Business Review* (Sept.–Oct.): 80.

14. Ibid., pp. 80–81.

15. Computer Sciences Corporation (CSC), pp. 6–7.

16. Wonder, Jacquelyn, and Patricia Donovan. 1989. *The Flexibility Factor: Why People Who Thrive on Change are Successful, and How You Can Become One of Them.* New York: Doubleday, p. 6.

17. Patterson, Gregory A. 1995. Lands' End Kicks out Modern New Managers, Rejecting a Makeover. *The Wall Street Journal* (Apr. 3).

18. Jacob, Rahul. 1994. Why Some Customers Are More Equal Than Others. *Fortune* (Sept. 19): 216, 220.

19. Chilton and Weidenbaum, p. 8.

20. Quoted in Chilton and Weidenbaum, p. 10.

21. Toffler, Alvin and Heidi. 1995. *Creating a New Civilization: The Politics of the Third Wave.* Atlanta: Turner Publishing, pp. 11, 52.

22. Stalk, George, Jr., and Thomas M. Hout. 1990. *Competing Against Time: How Time-Based Competition Is Reshaping Global Markets.* New York: Macmillan/The Free Press, pp. 76–77.

23. Toffler and Toffler, p. 38.

24. Krantz, Matt. 1995. Mead Is Testing the Limits of Automation. *Investor's Business Daily* (Feb. 1).

Chapter 4: Beginning-to-End Accountability

1. Rockart and Short, p. 7

2. Hogbin and Thomas, p. 5.

3. Ibid., p. 215.

4. Marshall, Edward M. 1995. *Transforming the Way We Work: The Power of the Collaborative Workplace.* New York: AMACOM, p. 61–62.

5. Cleland, David I. 1996. *Strategic Management of Teams.* New York: John Wiley, p. 90.

6. Brooks. *The Mythical Man-Month.* Anniversary ed., 216–17.

7. Computer Sciences Corporation (CSC), pp. 7, 10, 13.

8. Cusumano, Michael A. 1997. How Microsoft Makes Large Teams Work Like Small Teams. *Sloan Management Review* (Fall): 12–13.

9. Brooks. 1986. No Silver Bullet reprint, p. 185.

10. Center for Project Management. 1992–95. *Project Management Survey Analysis.* San Ramon, CA, p. 2.

11. Archibald. 1992. *Managing High-Technology Programs and Projects.* 2d ed. New York: John Wiley, p. 84.

12. Cash, McFarlan, and McKenney, p. 147.

13. Stuckenbruck, Linn C., ed. 1981. *The Implementation of Project Management: The Professional's Handbook.* Reading, MA: Addison-Wesley, p. 19.

14. Bedell, Gene. 1995. The Toughest Job Around. *Information Week* (Dec. 11): 136.

15. Hogbin and Thomas, p. 195.

16. U. S. General Accounting Office. 1994. *Improving Mission Performance through Strategic Information Management and Technology: Learning from Leading Organizations,* GAO/AIMD 94–115. Washington, DC. (May): 16.

17. Ibid., p.17.

18. Rockart and Short, p. 15.

19. Brooks. *The Mythical Man-Month.* Anniverary ed., p. 257.

20. Ibid., p. 256.

21. Wang, Charles B. 1997. *Techno Vision II.* Rev. ed. of Techno Vision. New York: McGraw-Hill, p. x.

Chapter 5: Cross-Boundary Coordination and Information Systems Division Home Departments

1. DeMarco, Tom. 1995. *Why Does Software Cost So Much?: And Other Puzzles of the Information Age.* New York: Dorset House, p. 209–10.

2. Beckard, Richard, and Reuben T. Harris. 1987. *Organizational Transitions: Managing Complex Change.* 2d ed. Reading, MA: Addison-Wesley, p. 51.

3. Krantz.

4. Galbraith, Jay R. 1994. *Competing with Flexible Lateral Organizations.* 2d ed. Reading, MA: Addison-Wesley, p. 6.

5. Ibid., p. 88.

6. Lawrence, Paul R., and Jay W. Lorsch. 1986. *Organization and Environment: Managing Differentiation and Integration.* Boston: Harvard Business School Press, pp. 65–66.

7. Rossmoore, Don. 1995. The Perils of Democracy. *Information Week* (Nov. 6): 168.

8. Grove, Andrew S. 1983. *High Output Management.* New York: Random House, p. 135.

9. Davis, Stanley M., and Paul R. Lawrence. 1977. *Matrix.* Reading, MA: Addison-Wesley, p. 107.

10. Grindley, Kit. 1995. *Managing I.T. at Board Level.* 2d ed. London: Pitman Publishing, p. 213–14.

11. McGinnis, Alan Loy. 1985. *Bringing Out the Best in People.* Minneapolis, MN: Augsburg Publishing House, p. 39.

12. Brooks, Frederick P., Jr. *The Mythical Man-Month.* Anniversary ed., p. 277.

13. McGinnis, p. 10.

14. Bashein, Barbara J., and M. Lynne Markus. 1997. A Credibility Equation for IT Specialists. *Sloan Management Review* (Summer): 36.

15. Pitts, Carl E. 1990. For Project Managers: An Inquiry into the Delicate Art and Science of Influencing Others. *Project Management Journal* (Mar.): 22.

16. Bashein and Markus, pp. 36–38.

17. Rockart and Short, pp. 14–15.

18. Quoted in Curtis, Bill, William E. Hefley, and Sally Miller. 1995. *People Capability Maturity Model,* Draft Version 0.3. Pittsburgh, PA: Software Engineering Institute, Carnegie Mellon University. (Apr.): 1.

19. Garner, Rochelle. 1995. Your Next Excellent Adventure. *Computerworld* (Sept. 11): 92.

20. Brooks. *The Mythical Man-Month.* Anniversary ed., p. 256.

21. de Bono, p. 225.

22. Bleichner, Gayle C., and Mary Pat Collins. 1995. An Organization Approach to Contract Resource Fulfillment. *Project Management Journal* (June): 46–51.

23. Garner. Your Next Excellent Adventure. p. 89.

24. Ibid., p. 92.

25. Quoted in Garner. Your Next Excellent Adventure, p. 92.

26. Garner. 1997. Still an Excellent Adventure? *Computerworld* (Mar. 31): 81.

27. Verity, John W. 1996. Let's Order Out for Technology. *Business Week* (May 13): 47.

28. Lacity, Mary C., Leslie P. Willcocks, and David F. Feeny. 1996. The Value of Selective IT Sourcing. Sloan Management Review (Spring): 22.

Chapter 6: The Management Reporting System

1. Anthony, Robert N. 1988. *The Management Control Function.* Boston: Harvard Business School Press, p. 135.

2. Thamhain, Hans J. 1996. Using Stage-Gate Reviews for Accelerating Product Development Projects. Project Management Institute 27th Annual Seminar/Symposium, Boston, Oct. 7–9. Upper Darby, PA: Project Management Institute, pp. 2–3.

3. Scotto, Marie. 1994. Project Budgeting: The Key to Bringing Business Projects in on Time and on Budget. *Project Management Journal* (Mar.): 35.

4. Fleming, Quentin W., and Joel M. Koppelman. 1995. Earned Value: Monitoring Performance against the Baseline. *PM Network* (Sept.): 9–10.

5. ———. 1996. *Earned Value Project Management.* Upper Darby, PA: Project Management Institute, p. 113.

6. Archibald. 1993. Re-Tooling the Project-Driven Organization. *PM Network* (Nov.): 7.

7. Whitten, Neal. 1995. *Managing Software Development Projects: Formula for Success.* 2d ed. New York: John Wiley, p. 213.

8. Ibid., p. 218.

Chapter 7: Creating the Operating and Project Concepts

1. Maglitta, Joseph E. 1997. Beyond ROI. *Computerworld* (Oct. 27): 73.

2. Senge, Peter M. 1990. *The Fifth Discipline: The Art & Practice of the Learning Organization.* New York: Doubleday/Currency, p. 342.

3. Quoted in Couger, J. Daniel. 1995. *Creative Problem Solving and Opportunity Finding.* Danvers, MA: boyd & fraser, p. 176.

4. Grindley, p. 87.

5. Quoted in Couger, p. 231.

6. Glass, Robert L. 1991. *Software Conflict: Essays on the Art and Science of Software Engineering.* Englewood Cliffs, NJ: Yourdon Press, p. 27.

Chapter 8: Project Execution Focus

1. Nadler and Hibino, p. 163.

2. Brooks, Frederick P., Jr. 1975. *The Mythical Man-Month: Essays on Software Engineering.* Reading, MA: Addison-Wesley, p. 153.

Index

Definition of Terms

advanced information technology: 2

concept: 9, 139

context: 14

development path: 146–147

goals and objectives: 18–19

initiative: 17

scope management: 43

TPP initiative: 16

Transformational Project Paradigm: 10–13

A

accountability: See also execution

accountability, continuing: See continuing accountability

accountability, lack of beginning-to-end: 81

accountability, and line ownership: See line ownership and accountability

accountability, dividing of: 74

accountability, maintaining: 165, 167

accountability, project 50, 103

accountability, separate: See separate accountability

accountability, split project: See split project accountability

actual progress to plan: 130

alignment: 53, 72–73, 99, 134, 154, 169, 174

alignment issue: 10

allocation of work: 80, 98

American Management Association survey: 65

annual budget: 46, 127, 128

application packages: 35, 88, 91, 151

applied creativity: 88, 117

architecture: 14, 32, 115, 119, 121, 172

assumptions: 48

audience, intended: 1

authority to refuse acceptance: 157

B

Bain & Co. study: 65

Bell-Atlantic: 40–41

board of directors: 82, 83, 148, 173

Boston Consulting Group: 66

budget, annual: See annual budget

budgetary control, loss of: See loss of budgetary control

budgeting and cost control: 80

budgeting in retrospect: 126

business area project ownership: 81

business value-added method: 142–143

R

S

U

UPGRADE YOUR PROJECT MANAGEMENT KNOWLEDGE WITH FIRST CLASS PUBLICATIONS FROM PMI

A Guide to the Project Management Body of Knowledge

The basic management reference for everyone who works on projects. Serves as a tool for learning about the generally accepted knowledge and practices of the profession. As "management by projects" becomes more and more a recommended business practice worldwide, the *PMBOK Guide* becomes an essential source of information that should be on every manager's bookshelf. Available in hardcover or paperback, the *PMBOK Guide* is an official standards document of the Project Management Institute.

ISBN: 1-880410-12-5 (paperback), 1-880410-13-3 (hardcover)

Interactive PMBOK Guide

This CD-ROM makes it easy for you to access the valuable information in PMI's *A Guide to the Project Management Body of Knowledge*. Features hypertext links for easy reference—simply click on underlined works in the text, and the software will take you to that particular section in the *PMBOK Guide*. Minimum system requirements: 486 PC, 8MB RAM, 10MB free disk space, CD-ROM drive, mouse or other pointing device, and Windows 3.1 or greater.

PMBOK Review Package

This "Box of Books" offers you a set of materials that supplements the *PMBOK Guide* in helping you develop a deeper understanding of the Project Management Body of Knowledge. These important and authoritative publications offer the depth and breadth you need to learn more about all the *PMBOK Guide* knowledge areas. Includes the following titles: *Project Management: A Managerial Approach; Project Planning, Scheduling & Control; Human Resource Skills for the Project Manager; Project and Program Risk Management; Quality Management for Projects & Programs; PMBOK Q&A; Managing the Project Team; Organizing Projects for Success;* and *Principles of Project Management.*

Managing Projects Step-by-Step™

Follow the steps, standards, and procedures used and proven by thousands of professional project managers and leading corporations. This interactive multimedia CD-ROM based on PMI's *A Guide to the Project Management Body of Knowledge* will enable you to customize, standardize, and distribute your project plan standards, procedures, and methodology across your entire organization. Multimedia illustrations using 3-D animations and audio make this perfect for both self-paced training or for use by a facilitator.

PMBOK Q&A

Use this handy pocket-sized question-and-answer study guide to learn more about the key themes and concepts presented in PMI's international standard, *A Guide to the Project Management Body of Knowledge*. More than 160 multiple-choice questions with answers (referenced to the *PMBOK Guide*) help you with the breadth of knowledge needed to understand key project management concepts.

ISBN: 1-880410-21-4

PMI Proceedings Library CD-ROM

This interactive guide to PMI's Annual Seminars & Symposium Proceedings offers a powerful new option to the traditional methods of document storage and retrieval, research, training, and technical writing. Contains complete paper presentations from PMI '91–PMI '97. Full text-search capability, convenient on-screen readability, and PC/Mac compatibility.

PMI Publications Library CD-ROM

Using state-of-the-art technology, PMI offers complete articles and information from its major publications on one CD-ROM, including *PM Network* (1991–97), *Project Management Journal* (1991–97), and *A Guide to the Project Management Body of Knowledge*. Offers full text-search capability and indexing by *PMBOK Guide* knowledge areas. Electronic indexing schemes and sophisticated search engines help to find and retrieve articles quickly that are relevant to your topic or research area.

ALSO AVAILABLE FROM PMI

Leadership Skills for Project Managers
Editors' Choice Series
Edited by Jeffrey Pinto and Jeffrey Trailer
ISBN: 1-880410-49-4

The Virtual Edge
Margery Mayer
ISBN: 1-880410-16-8

ABCs of DPC
PMI's Design-Procurement-Construction Specific Interest Group
ISBN: 1-880410-07-9

Project Management Casebook
Edited by David Cleland, Karen Bursic, Richard Puerzer, and A. Yaroslav Vlasak
ISBN: 1-880410-45-1

Project Management Casebook Instructor's Manual
Edited by David Cleland, Karen Bursic, Richard Puerzer, and A. Yaroslav Vlasak
ISBN: 1-880410-18-4

PMI Book of Project Management Forms
Spiral bound
ISBN: 1-880410-31-1
Diskette: 1-880410-50-8

Principles of Project Management
John Adams et al.
ISBN: 1-880410-30-3

Organizing Projects for Success
Human Aspects of Project Management Series, Volume 1
Vijay Verma
ISBN: 1-880410-40-0

Human Resource Skills for the Project Manager
Human Aspects of Project Management Series, Volume 2
Vijay Verma
ISBN: 1-880410-41-9

Managing the Project Team
Human Aspects of Project Management Series, Volume 3
Vijay Verma
ISBN: 1-880410-42-7

Earned Value Project Management
Quentin Fleming, Joel Koppelman
ISBN: 1-880410-38-9

Value Management Practice
Michel Thiry
ISBN: 1-880410-14-1

Decision Analysis in Projects
John Schuyler
ISBN: 1-880410-39-7

The World's Greatest Project
Russell Darnall
ISBN: 1-880410-46-X

Power & Politics in Project Management
Jeffrey Pinto
ISBN: 1-880410-43-5

Best Practices of Project Management Groups in Large Functional Organizations
Frank Toney, Ray Powers
ISBN: 1-880410-05-2

Project Management in Russia
Vladimir I. Voropajev
ISBN: 1-880410-02-8

Experience, Cooperation and the Future: The Global Status of the Project Management Profession
ISBN: 1-880410-04-4

A Framework for Project and Program Management Integration
R. Max Wideman
ISBN: 1-880410-01-X

Quality Management for Projects & Programs
Lewis R. Ireland
ISBN: 1-880410-11-7

Project & Program Risk Management
R. Max Wideman
ISBN: 1-880410-06-0